JAGDPANTHER VS 17-PDR ACHILLES

North-West Europe 1944–45

FRANK BALDWIN

OSPREY PUBLISHING
Bloomsbury Publishing Plc
Kemp House, Chawley Park, Cumnor Hill, Oxford OX2 9PH, UK
Bloomsbury Publishing Ireland Limited,
29 Earlsfort Terrace, Dublin 2, Ireland
1385 Broadway, 5th Floor, New York, NY 10018, USA
E-mail: info@ospreypublishing.com
www.ospreypublishing.com

OSPREY is a trademark of Osprey Publishing Ltd

First published in Great Britain in 2025

A catalogue record for this book is available from the British Library.

ISBN: PB 9781472862716; eBook 9781472862723;
ePDF 9781472862730; XML 9781472862747

25 26 27 28 29   10 9 8 7 6 5 4 3 2 1

Artwork by Richard Chasemore and Jim Laurier (page 30)
Maps and diagrams by bounford.com
Index by Rob Munro
Typeset by PDQ Digital Media Solutions, Bungay, UK
Printed by Repro India Ltd.

Osprey Publishing supports the Woodland Trust, the UK's leading woodland
conservation charity.

To find out more about our authors and books visit
www.ospreypublishing.com. Here you will find extracts, author interviews,
details of forthcoming events and the option to sign up for our newsletter.

For product safety related questions contact productsafety@bloomsbury.com

Acknowledgements

This book could not have been published without the expertise and support of
Nick Reynolds, my commissioning editor at Osprey Publishing. I am grateful
to The Tank Museum, the archives of which have been invaluable, and to The
Weald Foundation, which commented on the practical issues of running a
Jagdpanther. I owe thanks to the online elves who contribute to ww2talk.
com/, the internet forum dedicated to the British and Commonwealth
experience of World War II, and on https://forum.axishistory.com/; these sites
have been an invaluable sounding board and research resource. I am
particularly grateful to fellow battlefield historian Edwin Popken who found
and photographed the battle site. Finally, I owe everything to the patience,
tolerance and good humour of my wife Helen.

Author's note

Military-history enthusiasts widely know the M10 self-propelled gun armed
with the 17-pdr as the Achilles. During World War II, however, its official title
was the 17 Pounder SP M10. It was technically an artillery piece and followed
the rules for naming artillery equipment. Occasionally, this AFV was referred
to as the M10c, in the same way that the 17-pdr Sherman tanks were the 'c'
variant of the various M4 marks in British service. In 65 AT Regt RA, it was
known as the 'Mayfly'. The first official mention of the name 'Achilles' appears
to be in a Ministry of Supply document in April 1945.

Editor's note

All measurements of the angle of armour in this book are expressed in degrees
from vertical.

Title-page photograph: Soldiers of 56 Bty, 6 AT Regt RCA, are pictured at
Petawawa, Ontario, Canada, on 14 April 1943. Many of these men would still
be with the battery at the start of February 1945. (Kawartha Lakes Public
Library Digital Archive)

Glossary

AFV	Armoured Fighting Vehicle(s)
AP	Armour Piercing
APC	Armour Piercing Capped
APCBC	Armour Piercing Capped Ballistic Cap
APCR	Armour Piercing Composite Rigid
APDS	Armour Piercing Discarding Sabot
DS	Discarding Sabot
EK	*Eisernes Kreuz* (Iron Cross)
FlaK	*Flugzeugabwehrkanone* (anti-aircraft gun)
GMC	Gun Motor Carriage
HE	High Explosive
HE-HC-T	High Explosive, High Capacity – Tracer
HE-T	High Explosive – Tracer
HVAP	High Velocity Armour Piercing
KwK	*Kampfwagenkanone* (tank gun)
OP	Observation post
PaK	*Panzerabwehrkanone* (anti-tank gun)
QF	Quick Firing
RA	Royal Artillery
RCA	Royal Canadian Artillery
RHAe	Rolled Homogenous Armour equivalency

CONTENTS

INTRODUCTION

The 17-pdr M10 and the Jagdpanther were never intended to fight each other. Indeed, it was rare that they did. Although both were built to be anti-tank weapons, however, they did meet in combat occasionally, giving us the chance to compare the thinking behind their designs and the ways in which they were intended to be used as well as what happened when they met.

Both were radically different designs. The Jagdpanther was an armoured box on tracks mounting a big gun in a casemate with limited traverse. Other AFVs look a bit like it. One of the first French tanks, the *Saint-Chamond* introduced in April 1917, has a similar configuration. The Jagdpanther's configuration is shared with the German *Sturmgeschütz* (assault gun) as well as other *Jagdpanzer* types such as the Hetzer, Jagdpanzer IV, Ferdinand and Jagdtiger. The Soviet SU series are configured similarly.

Conversely, the 17-pdr M10 is a big gun in a lightly armoured 360-degree mounting on a tank chassis. It shares this configuration with two other US tank destroyers, the M18 and M36. It is not dissimilar to the innovative self-propelled Birch Gun introduced by the British Army in 1925, which mounted an 18-pdr gun on a medium-tank chassis. The Birch Gun was an experiment, however, and was abandoned six years later, the victim of a belief in the British Army that such an innovation was unrequired, expensive and unnecessary. It was a solution to a problem that did not exist, in the minds of British Army officers of the time.

If the role of anti-tank guns could be fulfilled by such very different designs, there must have been more to the role than just the technology. The way the vehicles were to be used, i.e. doctrine and training, must also have played a part.

Before World War II there were several big ideas as to how technology would change the next war. The invention of the tank and its use in World War I appeared to offer a way to avoid repeating trench warfare with its associated heavy casualties and

Photographed in 2011, this Jagdpanther is displayed at the Imperial War Museum, Duxford. It is believed to be one of Major Erich Sattler's group from sPzJgAbt 559. Note the single-piece barrel and the *Nahverteidigungswaffe* (close-range grenade thrower) mounted in the roof. Three metal rods were welded to the roof in front of the loader's hatch to hold the tripod mount of the Em 0,9 mR *Entfernungsmesser* (rangefinder). (Tony Hisgett/Wikimedia/CC BY 2.0)

lack of progress. Radical thinkers such as as J.F.C. Fuller and B.H. Liddell Hart in Britain, Charles de Gaulle in France and Mikhail N. Tukhachevsky in the Soviet Union envisaged mechanized warfare, characterized by massed tanks making deep penetrations into enemy lines. Oswald Lutz and Heinz Guderian led the German thinking around the Panzer division, which would deliver stunning victories between 1939 and 1941 in Poland, France, the Low Countries and the Balkans, and deep penetration into European Russia. The German Panzer divisions were not purely a tank force, however, but a combined-arms force moving at the speed of the tanks. At the heart of the Panzer division was a tank regiment or brigade which was to be used en masse.

In the 1920s and 1930s, there had been some thinking about how best to defend against enemy armour. Field artillery could be given anti-tank tasks. Most armies developed 20–45mm cannons as anti-tank guns, operated by the infantry or artillery, with one of these arms having primary responsibility for anti-tank defence. Germany was the only combatant in World War II with extensive prior experience of facing massed tanks, which its armies suffered between 1916 and 1918. German anti-aircraft artillery equipment had a secondary role engaging ground targets and could be fitted with direct-fire sights and provided with suitable ammunition. During World War I the Germans found self-propelled anti-aircraft guns to be particularly useful weapons as an anti-tank reserve.

The German Army of the 1930s adopted a 3.7cm PaK anti-tank gun and fielded it as a company of six guns per infantry regiment, one battalion per division and extra anti-tank battalions at corps and army level. The guns were towed by motorized tractors, even within the infantry formations, providing a mobile anti-tank defence. Combat experience from the Spanish Civil War (1936–39) demonstrated that concealed anti-tank guns could take a toll on tanks and that in the attack, anti-tank guns could provide infantry with light-artillery support. The Germans also identified a need for a heavy anti-tank gun to deal with heavy tanks or bunkers such as those of the French Maginot Line and Czech border defences. Experimental units were formed with towed and self-propelled 8.8cm guns. German innovation in self-propelled anti-tank guns was driven by confronting enemy tanks fitted with armour that could not be penetrated by the rounds fired by 3.7cm tank and anti-tank guns. The German Army's 3.7cm PaK was given the dismissive nickname of *Türklopf* ('door knocker') in recognition of its lack of armour penetration.

In 1940–41 the German Army commissioned 202 Panzerjäger I, mounting the Czech 4.7cm KPUV vz. 38 gun on the obsolescent PzKpfw I light-tank chassis, to tackle the French Char B1 bis heavy infantry tank. The shock of facing the Red Army's T-34 medium and KV-1 heavy tanks in 1941 prompted further German improvisation, with high-velocity 7.5cm and 7.62cm guns fitted in lightly armoured superstructures on obsolete or captured tanks. These proved invaluable in the steppes of southern Russia and the deserts of North Africa in 1942 where effective long-range anti-tank fire offered a critical advantage. These improvisations gave German forces the firepower to tackle Soviet and British tanks, but their crews were vulnerable to small-arms fire or shell splinters.

At the same time, the Germans were expanding their use and production of the Sturmgeschütz III, which mounted a gun or howitzer in an armoured casemate on the PzKpfw III medium-tank chassis. These AFVs were under the control of the artillery arm and were intended to provide mobile, armoured close-support artillery to aid infantry formations. There was a political element to the formation of the assault artillery. The debate about whether tanks should be parcelled out to support the infantry or concentrated in armoured formations had been won by the Panzer arm. As a result, German tanks were organized in the Panzer and Light divisions. The *Sturmgeschütze* fulfilled the function of infantry-support tanks, but were outside the control of the Panzer arm. Initially armed with a low-velocity 7.5cm StuK 37 L/24 gun, the Sturmgeschütz III's main armament was replaced by higher-velocity 7.5cm StuK 40 L/43 or L/48 guns. Over the course of World War II, the design of the Sturmgeschütz III and IV converged with that of the *Jagdpanzer*, with both mounting a high-velocity 7.5cm gun in an armoured casemate on a PzKpfw III or PzKpfw IV medium-tank chassis.

The first 8.8cm self-propelled gun, mounting a FlaK 18 anti-aircraft gun on an SdKfz 8 half-track chassis, could deal with concrete bunkers or fortress turrets, its anticipated targets, but would also overmatch any Allied tank in the early-war years. Ten were manufactured and served with an anti-tank unit until the final three were knocked out in 1943. The Germans also developed experimental self-propelled heavy guns mounted on tank chassis as anti-fortification weapons. Two prototypes were developed for both the 10.5cm K gepanzerte Selbstfahrlafette, nicknamed *Dicker* [Fat] *Max*, mounting a 10.5cm schwere Kanone 18 on a PzKpfw IV chassis, and the 12.8cm Selbstfahrlafette auf VK 30.01(H), aka *Sturer* [Stubborn] *Emil*,

mounting a 12.8cm Kanone 40 L/61 gun (based on the 12.8cm FlaK 40) on a Henschel VK 30.01(H) heavy-tank chassis. None of the four prototypes were used in their intended role, but all four were employed as anti-tank guns on the Eastern Front.

In the continuing search for long-range anti-tank guns, the Germans sought to mount the 8.8cm gun in self-propelled chassis during 1942. Two such projects were developed. The Hornisse/Nashorn (Hornet/Rhino) tank destroyer mounted an 8.8cm PaK 43/1 anti-tank gun in a lightly armoured superstructure on a chassis built from PzKpfw III and IV tanks; 494 were manufactured. The Panzerjäger Tiger (P) tank destroyer, initially christened Ferdinand after its designer, Dr Ferdinand Porsche, and later re-named Elefant, mounted an 8.8cm PaK 43/2 anti-tank gun on the redundant chassis of the unsuccessful Porsche design for the Tiger tank; 91 were built. These were interim solutions, however, as the Hornisse/Nashorn was too small and lightly armoured and the Ferdinand too heavy. Meanwhile the Red Army was introducing more heavily armed and armoured tanks and self-propelled guns such as the KV-85 heavy tank, 85mm SU-85 self-propelled gun and 152mm SU-152 self-propelled heavy howitzer and was deploying armour en masse as tank corps. This was the rationale for the development of the Jagdpanther.

In the British Army, the Royal Artillery was responsible for manning and coordinating anti-tank defence. Field artillery had been assigned an anti-tank role since 1918. The British Army adopted the Ordnance QF 2-pdr (40mm) anti-tank gun in 1935, but did not form specialist anti-tank regiments until 1938. British anti-tank doctrine was essentially defensive, with the sole task of providing close

An Achilles IIc, the 17-pdr-armed variant reaching the front lines towards the end of the Normandy fighting. Note the omission of the bolted fittings for additional armour. (Tank Museum 2999-E1)

support to the other arms in all phases of war. In the advance, anti-tank guns were to protect attackers from armoured counter-attacks. In the event, there were far too few British anti-tank units to deal with the imminent onslaught of the German Panzer divisions. After the Dunkirk evacuation (26 May–4 June 1940), the British commissioned the Bartholomew Committee to investigate the lessons to be drawn from the recent fighting in Belgium and France. The subsequent report recommended a substantial increase in the number of anti-tank guns, including the provision of corps-level anti-tank regiments, and that a proportion of anti-tank guns in infantry divisions should be mounted on armoured, self-propelled chassis. Although there was some support in the British Army for the concept of using self-propelled anti-tank guns aggressively as tank destroyers, the General Staff role as published envisaged a more defensive role. The development of the British Army's anti-tank practice was heavily influenced by the experience of fighting in North Africa.

Unfortunately for the British Army, its biggest problem was replacing the equipment lost at Dunkirk. It would take 18 months before it was able to introduce new anti-tank equipment. The initial self-propelled anti-tank gun was a 2-pdr anti-tank gun mounted on a Loyd Carrier, but this combination was never produced in significant numbers. After Dunkirk, most British combat took place in North Africa during mobile desert battles in which engagements occurred at ranges for which the 2-pdr was ineffective against German tank armour. Widespread use was made of 2-pdr anti-tank guns mounted 'en portee' on unarmoured 15cwt trucks, which provided mobility but at suicidal levels of protection. Only in mid-1942 were the British able to replace the obsolete 2-pdr with Ordnance QF 6-pdr (57mm) anti-tank guns.

The self-propelled version of the 6-pdr, the Mk I Gun Carrier, known as the Deacon, was introduced into the anti-tank regiments in armoured divisions in September 1942. The gun was mounted in an armoured turret on an AEC Matador 4×4 truck chassis with an armoured cab; but while the Deacon provided mobility, it was difficult to conceal or dig in. The British were successful in defeating German armour at Alam el Halfa, Egypt (30 August–5 September 1942), and Medenine Pass, Tunisia (6 March 1943), by setting anti-tank ambushes with heavy belts of 6-pdr guns around killing zones. The British introduced the Ordnance QF 17-pdr (76.2mm) anti-tank gun in early 1943, rushing its introduction to face the Tiger heavy tanks expected to be encountered in Tunisia.

In December 1942 the decision was made that the British Army would adopt the US M10 tank destroyer mounting a 3in M7 gun. The M10 had been adopted by the US Army as a self-propelled tank destroyer to equip its Tank Destroyer Force, a new arm with an ethos to take an aggressive mobile response to counter enemy tank thrusts. In 1940, the German success against the French Army – supposedly the best in the world – was a big shock to the US Army. The impression of columns of tanks supported by dive bombers was the basis for the Blitzkrieg legend. The US Army's response to the German Blitzkrieg was to create the Tank Destroyer Force.

The tank-destroyer concept was a US Army idea developed before the Japanese attack on Pearl Harbor (7 December 1941). The US Army sought anti-tank weapons that could be used aggressively and offensively against anticipated massed German armour. In 1941, Major (later General) Albert C. Wedemeyer, a graduate of the

A view of the breech of the Jagdpanther's 8.8cm main gun. The racking on the right would hold the 8.8cm rounds. The square hatch at the rear of the casemate facilitated access to the main gun. (Weald Foundation)

German Kriegsakademie (War Academy), proposed a train of development in an article published simultaneously in May 1941 by *Infantry Journal* and *Field Artillery Journal* (Wedemeyer 1941). Given the tendency of German Panzer divisions to mass rapidly against a selected point of the defender's line, Wedemeyer considered it vital that anti-tank forces should also be capable of concentrating in critical areas of the front. 'The bulk of antitank units [should] therefore [be] pooled in G.H.Q.,' held in highly mobile, centrally located three-battalion groups, and attached to the field armies and corps threatened by tank attack. He proposed that the primary weapon of these formations should be mobile, heavily armed 'tank chasers' and suggested that medium tanks might fulfil that role.

The US Army tested different anti-tank weapons from 37mm to 105mm calibre mounted on wheeled and half-tracked platforms, all referred to as 'tank destroyers'. While the T24 and M40, both armed with a 3in gun, never saw active service, the M6 GMC – a 37mm M3 anti-tank gun mounted on a Dodge WC52 truck, intended as a stopgap for training – and the M3 GMC, mounting a 75mm M1897 anti-tank gun mounted on a half-track, fought in Tunisia during 1943. The first major combat between US and German forces was at Kasserine Pass (18–24 February 1943) and put the US Army's tank-destroyer doctrine to the test, which it did not pass. By 1943 the Germans were not making massed tank attacks, but advancing cautiously with combined-arms teams, with artillery engaging enemy anti-tank guns. The only US Army tank-destroyer equipment to perform well was the M10.

By early 1943 the British 6-pdr anti-tank gun was being supplemented by the 17-pdr anti-tank gun as towed equipment in the British Army. The tactical requirements for British anti-tank guns had changed as the open battlefields of the Western Desert gave way to the closer terrain of Europe. Furthermore, the onus would be on the Allies to attack. As one report from Italy put it: 'The greatest difficulty the infantry will face is in overcoming the enemy's counter-attack which must be expected within a few hours of their assault and which will include armour. The attacking infantry must get up their own supporting anti-tank weapons – but this is often extremely difficult to do quickly and before the counter-attack comes' (DO 7 Armd Div 2021/5/G, 17 October 1943). The same report recommended a strong anti-tank framework so designed that the guns were defiladed from the enemy with a close and killing shoot for the 6-pdr and a long shoot for the 17-pdr, with the latter used for breaking up tank attacks at long range. At the same time, there was dissatisfaction within the Royal Artillery about the lack of a decent gun tractor for the 17-pdr towed equipment combining towing power with survivability in forward areas.

In September 1942 a General Staff specification for a self-propelled 17-pdr anti-tank gun with all-round traverse was sent to the Ministry of Supply and a design based on the A30 Challenger cruiser-tank chassis was ordered. By this time, however, it was easier to fulfil the requirement by mounting the 17-pdr in the M10. Thus, the 17-pdr M10 and Jagdpanther arose from rather different tactical imperatives, although both were intended to knock out the heaviest enemy armour at a range of 1,500m or more. The former was to provide mobile long-range fire as the initial long-range support following an infantry attack, while the latter was intended to break up attacks by massed enemy armour.

CHRONOLOGY

1939
1 September   Germany invades Poland. Start of World War II in Europe.

1940
10 May   Start of the German assault on France and the Low Countries, which demonstrates the power of Blitzkrieg based on air power and tanks.

1941
22 June   The Axis invasion of the Soviet Union commences.

1942
December   The British Army decides to adopt the M10 tank destroyer.

1943
February   The M10 tank destroyer makes its debut with US Army forces in Tunisia.
5 July   The Panther medium tank is first used in combat at Kursk in Operation *Zitadelle*.
3 August   Jagdpanther development begins, using the Panther chassis and the 8.8cm PaK 43 anti-tank gun.
20 October   The first Jagdpanther prototype is delivered.

1944
January   MIAG begins producing the Jagdpanther.
6 June   The D-Day Allied landings in Normandy: 24 17-pdr M10s land with British Second Army.
9 July   17-pdr SP M10s from 245 Bty RA knock out 13 German tanks in the battle for Caen.
30 July   The Jagdpanther makes its combat debut in Normandy as schwere Panzerjäger-Abteilung 554 knocks out 11 Churchill tanks.

1945
8 February   Operation *Veritable*, the Anglo-Canadian attack on the Reichswald, begins.
11 February   Duel between a 17-pdr M10c of 56 AT Bty RCA and a Jagdpanther of schwere Panzerjäger-Abteilung 655.
March   Jagdpanther production ceases.
8 May   German forces surrender in the West.

A valuable glimpse of the rear hull storage of a 17-pdr of 75 AT Regt RA (11th Armoured Division) near Deurne in the the Netherlands, 11 October 1944. (Tank Museum 3000-C5)

DESIGN AND DEVELOPMENT

By the middle of World War II there was a broad consensus among the combatants about tank design. Tanks had an armoured body and a tracked chassis with the main armament mounted in an armoured turret. There was, however, far less consensus about the design of self-propelled anti-tank guns, tank destroyers or tank hunters. These AFVs sacrificed some degree of mobility or protection to incorporate a bigger main gun than could be mounted on the tank chassis available.

One way to achieve this was to mount the main armament on top of the chassis with limited protection for the crew. Many self-propelled guns were based on obsolete or obsolescent tanks; for example, the German 4.7cm Panzerjäger I, and the Marder series mounting a 7.5cm or 7.62cm gun on tanks that originally mounted a 2cm or 3.7cm gun, as did the captured French AFVs converted by Baukommando *Becker*. The British and Americans also tried this approach, while the Red Army fielded the open-topped SU-76M self-propelled gun in large numbers.

A second approach was to mount the main gun in an armoured casemate instead of a turret, retaining protection at the expense of a limited traverse. This was the concept behind the Soviet SU-85 tank destroyer, the German *Sturmgeschütz* assault gun and the British 3in Churchill Gun Carrier. This solution also meant such vehicles had a lower silhouette, making them harder to hit. Towards the end of World War II, more and more German AFVs followed this pattern. The Marder series of open-topped *Panzerjäger* were supplemented with the enclosed Jagdpanzer 38 (SdKfz 138/2) 'Hetzer', Jagdpanzer IV (SdKfz 162) and of course the Jagdpanther (SdKfz 173).

M10 ACHILLES

The 17-pdr SP M10 Achilles was a British modification of the US M10 GMC, replacing the 3in M7 gun with the British Ordnance QF 17-pdr. It retained the single .50-calibre M2 Browning heavy machine gun mounted on the rear of the turret. The M10 is not a tank. It emerged from the US Army's search for offensive anti-tank weapons to combat armoured forces under the direction of the Tank Destroyer Force.

By November 1941 the US Ordnance Department was becoming dissatisfied with the various anti-tank weapons trialled up to that point. As a consequence, it issued an additional specification for a tank destroyer with a 3in gun in a rotating turret. Design work started on the 3in GMC T35, which combined an early-production M4A2 medium tank hull with the 3in M7 gun from the M6 heavy tank in a cast, circular, open-topped turret. Based on combat reports from the fighting in the Philippines in 1941–42, the armour on the sides and rear of the upper hull was changed from flat to sloped plates. The test vehicle was designated the 3in GMC T35E1. Prototypes of the T35 and T35E were delivered to Aberdeen Proving Ground, Maryland, in April 1942. On 2 May 1942, the T35E1 was chosen for further development. The thickness of the T35E1's side and rear upper hull armour was reduced from 1in (25.4mm) to 0.75in (19mm) in order to reduce the vehicle's weight. Out of concern for the thinness of the armour, however, bosses for appliqué armour panels were added to the hull sides, glacis and turret sides. The turret design was changed to a sloped pentagonal shape made of welded armour plate, after concerns were raised about the difficulty of casting the turret.

On 2 May 1942, the Tank Destroyer Board agreed that the M10 would become the standard self-propelled tank destroyer in the US Army, despite reservations about

Pictured in January 2017, this 17-pdr Achilles is displayed alongside a standard M10 at the Third Cavalry Museum, Fort Hood, Texas. (Skaarup.HA/Wikimedia/ CC BY-SA 4.0)

its low speed (only 30mph) and high weight (32 tons). It was considered an interim expedient pending the development of a faster, smaller vehicle, which would emerge as the 76mm GMC M18, the Hellcat. The M10 first saw action in Tunisia on 23 March 1943, at the battle of El Guettar, which also saw the first test of US tank-destroyer doctrine. An alternative design, the 3in GMC M10A1 based on the M4A3 medium-tank chassis, was also authorized for production. This stemmed from a concern that production of M4A2 chassis would be inadequate for the numbers of M10 ordered.

The 3in GMC M10 is a modification of the standard M4A2 medium-tank chassis, mounting the 3in M7 gun in an open-top, hand-operated, 360-degree-traversable turret. The vehicle weighed 32 tons and carried a crew of five and 54 rounds of 3in ammunition. A 375hp (280kW) General Motors 6/71 Diesel Model 6046 'twin six' engine provided a top speed of 30mph, with a maximum grade-ability of 50 per cent. The fording depth is 36in. The 3in GMC M10A1 differs from the M10 only in its power plant: a 500hp (373kW) Ford GAA V-8 petrol engine providing approximately the same performance characteristics as those of the M10.

The M10's turret traverse was purely manual, taking around 80 seconds to traverse 180 degrees. Despite concerns that the vehicle was heavier than originally specified, weights were fitted to the turret rear to counter the weight of the barrel, which would have otherwise made it impossible to traverse the turret on any slope greater than 4 degrees. Initially, these were lead weights fitted into racks for track grousers. These weights were replaced by 3,700lb cast-iron wedges, added to production vehicles from 29 January 1943. These were, in turn replaced by a 'duck bill' design that overhung the turret rear further, but weighed only 2,500lb.

The .50-calibre M2 heavy machine gun mounted on the turret rear was a partial solution to the need for close-range firepower, but it was not enough on its own. In September 1943, a single M10 was fitted with the Oilgear hydraulic power-traverse system used in the M4 medium tank. It was not adopted, however, as by this time the production run of the M10 was nearly complete. There was no charging engine, so the main engine needed to be run occasionally to recharge the batteries, which would otherwise be drained by using the vehicle's radio.

The British Army had decided on the need for anti-tank guns on self-propelled mountings in their review of operations leading to the Dunkirk evacuation, published as the Bartholomew Report. As early as August 1940, the Director of Armoured Fighting Vehicles, Major-General V.V. Pope, asked for a self-propelled anti-tank gun for incorporation into armoured divisions. There was some support for the aggressive use of anti-tank guns like the US tank destroyers, but when a General Staff requirement was issued in September 1941 the role envisaged was purely defensive. The rationale for developing a self-propelled anti-tank gun stemmed from four requirements. First, to enable long marches to be carried out without detriment of the equipment. Second, to get better performance over rough country than could be obtained with a towed gun. Third, to provide a 'hit and run' weapon. Finally, to facilitate movement across country of reserve guns to threatened areas.

At that time, however, there were no British self-propelled anti-tank guns in development. Manufacturing capacity was focused on replacing losses incurred during 1940. In the Middle East, the British improvised 37mm and 2-pdr guns on the backs

17-pdr M10, 6 AT REGT RCA

This photograph shows the use of external stowage as per one manual, with a tarpaulin, camouflage net and blankets wrapped in groundsheets. In practice there was considerable variety in how personal kit was stored. (Tank Museum 2999-F6)

OPPOSITE
This artwork shows a 17-pdr M10 of 91 AT Regt RA, VIII Corps' anti-tank regiment. The vehicle has been portrayed with track extensions to provide better mobility in soft ground.

of locally converted Ford 30cwt trucks to enable the truck to take the shock of discharge and allow for nearly 360 degrees of traverse. This improvisation, known as the 2-pdr portee, offered the advantage of a quick getaway when British forces were withdrawing and provided a mobile reserve of anti-tank guns. A high silhouette and lack of protection rendered the 2-pdr portee vulnerable in battle, however. The posthumous Victoria Cross awarded to Second Lieutenant G.W. Gunn, who was killed in action manning a 2-pdr portee at Sidi Rezegh, Libya, on 21 November 1941, indicates the vulnerability of the gun crew.

During 1941 the British planned to introduce two new anti-tank guns. The 6-pdr had been commissioned in 1938, in anticipation of developments in tank armour. Production was delayed, however, in favour of manufacturing the existing 2-pdr to replace those lost in the retreat and evacuation from France. The 6-pdr appeared in service from the end of 1941. There was a self-propelled version, mounted in an armoured box structure on a 3-ton AEC Matador truck chassis and given the name Deacon. This was issued on a scale of one battery to each anti-tank regiment. The Deacon was not an unqualified success, however, owing to its size and the difficulty of digging it in and concealing it.

Arrangements were made to replace the Deacon in armoured divisions with the US 3in M10. An initial order for 1,500 M10s was placed and the first deliveries to the Middle East were made in June 1943. Some 1,648 M10s were delivered to the British. There was a problem, however: the 3in M7 gun was the only weapon of that calibre in British service, which caused logistics and training problems.

The second anti-tank gun under development in 1941 was the 17-pdr, the design for which was initiated by mid-April 1941. It was to have a muzzle velocity of 3,000ft/sec

and a penetrative capacity of 125mm (4.92in) at 600yd. There were concerns about the size of the equipment, but given the urgency posed by the likely appearance of German heavy tanks, an order was given to commence manufacture. A wooden mock-up was made by August 1941. There were difficulties in designing a carriage that could withstand the large recoil forces, however, with the result that ordnance was available before the carriages. The first 100 17-pdrs were hurriedly mounted on 25-pdr gun-howitzer carriages and shipped to Tunisia in early 1943 to counter German Tiger tanks.

Work was proceeding on a General Staff specification for a self-propelled 17-pdr with an all-round traverse, which was originally sent to the Ministry of Supply in September 1942. In summer 1943 various alternative mountings were considered and it was decided to use the A30 chassis similar to that of the Challenger tank, which might be available for issue in the second half of 1944. In the event, the earliest production models did not become available until December 1945. The Royal Artillery faced a further problem as this vehicle, the A30 Avenger, was classed as a tank and therefore came under the purview of the Royal Armoured Corps. The Royal Artillery also pursued a self-propelled 17-pdr mounted on the Valentine infantry-tank chassis in a fixed open mounting, which appeared as the Archer in late 1944.

In the meantime, it was found that the version of the M10 supplied to Britain had in fact been built to be capable of mounting different armament. The initial batches of M10s that were delivered had an easily modified gun mounting to allow for the future replacement of the older 3in M7 gun with the newer 76mm M1 gun or even a 105mm howitzer. This gun mounting design allowed the British to replace the 3in M7 gun with the 17-pdr gun. The latter could be fitted with minimal modifications, and so 1,100 M10s supplied to Britain were converted to mount the 17-pdr Mk V. Britain took delivery of some 845 vehicles in 1943, but of the second version of the M10, only the T71 mark designed to carry the M1 gun could carry the 17-pdr gun.

Converted vehicles were known as the 17-pdr SP M10, the M10c or, occasionally, the M10 Firefly. In early 1945 the name Achilles became official usage for the M10 in British service, the Mk I (the US M10) being powered by the General Motors 'twin six' diesel engine and the Mk II (the US M10A1) by the Ford V8 petrol engine. The M10 equipped with the 17-pdr gun was given the suffix 'c', e.g. Achilles Mk Ic.

The weight of the 17-pdr's breech meant that the gun required a counterweight to be fitted behind the muzzle brake on its long barrel to balance it in elevation. Thus the 17-pdr SP was counterweighted in each direction, which would have worried the US Army staff, who agonized about the excess weight. The muzzle brake and counterweight on the barrel also gave the Achilles a distinctive appearance compared to the comparatively short-barrelled, brakeless, entirely straight barrel of the M10. There was a concern that the Germans would target this equipment once they discovered the effectiveness of the 17-pdr gun. As a result, attempts were made to disguise the 17-pdr by painting its muzzle brake and counterweight, which can be seen in many contemporary photographs. There is no evidence, however, that the Germans were aware of the significance of the longer barrel on either the M10 or M4 Sherman medium tank, or that it influenced German targeting priorities.

Two other material changes were made to M10s supplied to Britain. First, armour plates 17mm (0.67in) thick were welded to the front and sides. Second, the British replaced the US radio with a No. 19 set. Additionally, on some M10s, the open turret

was fitted with a 20mm-thick shield to protect the crew from overhead threats as a local modification.

The British had planned to convert some 1,000 M10s into 17pdr-armed variants for the invasion of Normandy, but the conversion work was not started until April 1944. The British Army understood the delay was due to an industrial dispute. By 6 June, enough M10s had been converted to arm the self-propelled batteries of only two anti-tank regiments: 62 AT Regt RA (I Corps) and 73 AT Regt RA (XXX Corps). The low numbers of 17-pdr M10s available at the start of the invasion of Normandy meant that many British units went ashore fielding standard 3in M10s. The number of conversions per month increased, however, and by the end of 1944, some 790 M10s had undergone the necessary conversion work, 152 vehicles in November alone.

Pictured in 1950, this Achilles in Dutch service bears the name 'Leeuw' (Lion). Note the additional storage space between the counterweights and the turret. (Leger Film- en Fotodienst/Wikimedia/CC0)

Number of 3in M10 conversions to 17-pdr by month					
May 1944	98	September 1944	112	January 1945	86
June 1944	81	October 1944	126	February 1945	95
July 1944	69	November 1944	152	March 1945	30
August 1944	70	December 1944	82	April 1945	18
Source: Zaloga 2002: 21				**Total**	**1,019**

Thus a vehicle adopted as an interim expedient by the US Army Tank Destroyer Force and as an interim self-propelled 17-pdr by the British would prove to be the main British self-propelled anti-tank gun for the key Anglo-American operation of World War II – the Normandy landings. The M10's key strength was the ease with which the original 3in M7 gun could be replaced by the 17-pdr gun in British service and the 90mm M3 gun in US service to become the M36 tank destroyer.

OPPOSITE

This artwork depicts an early-model Jagdpanther as issued to schwere Panzerjäger-Abteilung 654 in summer 1944. It is finished in factory dark yellow and with equipment stowed on the sides before the vehicle was painted by the unit and equipment stowed on the rear deck.

JAGDPANTHER

The PzKpfw V Panther was one of World War II's most influential AFV designs. Regarded by many as the best medium tank of the conflict, the Panther strongly influenced post-war Western tank design. It was developed as the German answer to the unpleasant experience of facing the Soviet T-34 medium tank, which was better armed and armoured than any tank it fought against in 1941.

In early August 1942, the Heereswaffenamt, the German Army's ordnance department, requested Friedrich Krupp AG to submit designs for a new *Jagdpanzer*, or tank destroyer. It was to be armed with the 8.8cm PaK 43 anti-tank gun and based on the chassis of the Panther tank, at that time under development but not yet in production. Krupp designers claimed that construction drawings for the new *Jagdpanzer* could not be completed before January 1943, however. This delay may have been through a reluctance to forego work on their heavy *Sturmgeschütz*, commissioned in 1939. This meant that the *Jagdpanzer* design would not meet the specified delivery date of first production in June 1943, with full-scale production scheduled to begin the following month. As a result, the design work was passed to Daimler-Benz. The latter company's personnel met on 5 January 1943 in Berlin, to define what was then called the '8,8 cm Sturmgeschütz auf Panther Fahrgestell' (assault gun on a Panther chassis).

On 1 May 1943, the Heereswaffenamt issued specifications for the armour shape and thickness of a vehicle redesignated the '8,8 cm *Panzerjäger* 43/3 L/71 auf Panther Fahrgestell' (8.8cm Tank hunter 43/3 L/71 on Panther chassis). Daimler-Benz was tasked with taking over the design and development as production was to be undertaken by the company's Berlin-Marienfelde plant. The new AFV's chassis was to be based on that of the Panther II medium tank, including its 100mm frontal and 80mm side armour; but when the Panther II project was discontinued just three days

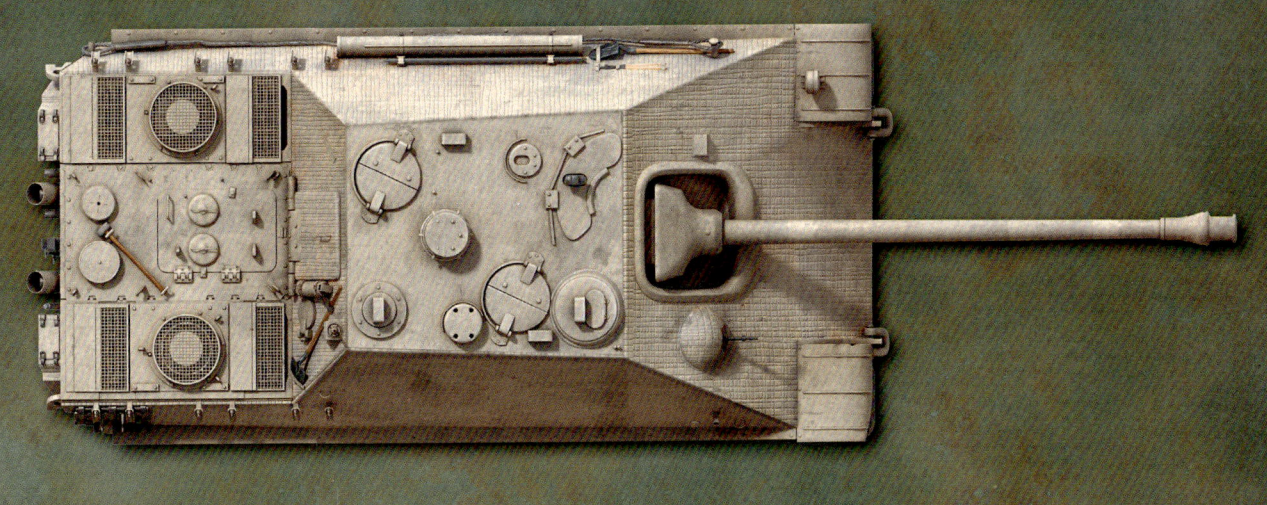

The Panther medium tank was the basis for the Jagdpanther. This example is pictured in July 1944 in Normandy. Both the Panther and the Jagdpanther had a formidable main gun and thick frontal armour. Both also required careful driving and maintenance. (Keystone-France/Gamma-Keystone via Getty Images)

later, the armour thicknesses were reduced to 80mm and 30mm respectively. The first hulls were to be ready by mid-1943.

Daimler-Benz lacked the space in its Berlin-Marienfelde works, however, and the decision was made on 23 May 1943 to hand over the manufacture and final design work to MIAG (Mühlenbau und Industrie Aktiengesellschaft) in Braunschweig. Daimler-Benz and MIAG demonstrated a full-size model of the new AFV before Hitler in October 1943. MIAG then built two prototypes, which were completed in October and November 1943. Production started at MIAG's Braunschweig plant in January 1944. The next month, Hitler specified the simpler name Jagdpanther instead of the cumbersome original. As a result of damage to the Braunschweig plant inflicted by Allied bombing raids, two additional companies' assembly plants were tasked: MNH (Maschinenfabrik Niedersachsen Hannover), which started production in November 1944; and MBA (Maschinenbau und Bahnbedarf) in Potsdam from December 1944. MIAG produced 270 Jagdpanthers, MNH 112 and MBA 33, for a total of 415.

The fixed casemate of the Jagdpanther was built up by extending the glacis plate and sloped hull sides of the Panther II chassis to provide a crew compartment big enough to serve the huge main gun and accommodate its large fixed ammunition. The side plates sloped at slightly less of an angle, and were thicker than the corresponding side plates on the Panther II. Other minor changes to armour thickness were also intended to maximize interior space. The lower frontal hull plate was reduced to 60mm (2.4in) although the upper hull frontal plate remained 80mm (3.1in). Changes to the chassis armour were also introduced with the Panther Ausf G on the main Panther assembly lines in spring 1944.

The Jagdpanther was armed with the 8.8cm PaK 43/3 L/71 gun, very similar to the main gun of the PzKpfw VIB Tiger II or *Königstiger* ('King Tiger') heavy tank. The gun was mounted in an armoured casemate with 12 degrees of traverse either side (Spielberger 2004: 188).

The Jagdpanther had a crew of five: commander, driver, radio operator/machine-gunner, gunner and loader. Its gun could destroy any type of tank the Jagdpanther was

OPPOSITE

This artwork shows a Jagdpanther completed in about November 1944. modelled on the vehicle that took part in the duel at the Dammershof. Note the welded loops for attaching foliage for camouflage.

JAGDPANTHER, LOW COUNTRIES, EARLY 1945

likely to face. Based on the Panther Ausf G chassis, the Jagdpanther had an acceptable power-to-weight ratio, and according to German sources the vehicle encountered few mechanical problems additional to those of the Panther. British tests on Jagdpanthers completed post-war reached a different conclusion, however. A group of tanks and tank destroyers was assembled under British supervision at the MNH plant using components on the assembly lines. Among the vehicles were 14 Jagdpanthers, two of which were tested along with two Panthers on the standard acceptance tests for British military vehicles. The tests were abandoned once all four vehicles had broken down and could not be repaired even after the casualties had been cannibalized. The conclusive report, dated February 1948, notes that 'very little information of any value was obtained', the reason being the 'general mechanical unreliability of the Panther and Jagdpanther tanks'. The Jagdpanther in the Tank Museum at Bovington, Dorset, is one of those built post-war.

The Jagdpanther had two primary variants, with changes implemented gradually over time. The earliest models, known as G1 1944, featured a small welded main-gun mantlet, a one-piece PaK 43/3 L/71 gun, a modified Panther Ausf A engine deck and two vision openings for the driver. As Jagdpanther production continued, a Panther Ausf G engine deck, a larger, externally bolted gun mantlet and a two-piece KwK 43/4 L/71 gun were incorporated. Zimmerit anti-magnetic paste was applied to the tank until September 1944, after which it was discontinued. While early Jagdpanthers had two vision openings for the driver, later versions had only one. The Jagdpanther's main gun originally had a monobloc gun barrel, but, from May 1944 onwards, this was gradually replaced by a more cost-effective two-part barrel after crews determined that barrel wear was uneven. The later examples of the Jagdpanther were identified as G2.

There were several projected developments of the Jagdpanther, none of which came to fruition. Friedrich-Krupp made a drawing showing the main armament upgunned to the 12.8cm PaK 80 L/55. After concerns about the slow rate of fire of the Panther compared to the Allied M4 medium tank, development work commenced on an autoloader for the 8.8cm PaK L71. Work was also started on a barrel blow-out device, i.e. a bore evacuator or fume extractor.

TECHNICAL SPECIFICATIONS

Any technical comparison between the 17-pdr M10 and the Jagdpanther needs to take into account the great disparity between these vehicles. The M10, adopted as an expedient, was a solution to a problem presented by the German armour of 1940–42. The Germans had already developed a range of *Panzerjäger* on a similar concept to the M10, mounting heavy anti-tank guns on lightly armoured tank chassis, namely the Marder series mounting 7.5cm and 7.62cm guns, and the Nashorn mounting the 8.8cm gun. These vehicles proved too underpowered or vulnerable, however. The next generation of *Jagdpanzer*, such as the 7.5cm Jagdpanzer IV, Hetzer and the 8.8cm Jagdpanther, would mount their armament in a heavily armoured casemate. All three were developed to meet the threat posed by increasingly heavily armed and armoured Soviet tanks emerging during the war years. The Western Allies would not have tanks comparable to those of the Red Army until 1945. The 8.8cm KwK 43 overmatched the Allied tanks.

A Jagdpanther crewman sprays paint on his vehicle, 1944. (Bundesarchiv, Bild 101I-721-0397-19/Wagner/CC BY-SA 3.0 de)

FIREPOWER

M10 Achilles

The 17-pdr was arguably the best British anti-tank gun developed during World War II. With its standard APCBC ammunition it was capable of penetrating most German tanks. The APDS rounds introduced in late 1944 offered improved penetration and presaged the anti-tank ammunition used by post-war tanks. Some contend that the US 90mm M3 gun mounted in the M36 tank destroyer was a better anti-tank gun than the 17-pdr, but the M3 was not available for the key battles in Normandy following D-Day.

According to one British source (WO 219/2806, Appx G; see below), the 17-pdr gun mounted on the M10 was able to penetrate around 127mm of armour at 600yd (548m) and 120mm at 1,000yd (914m) using standard APCBC ammunition impacting at a 30-degree angle. When supplied, APDS ammunition could penetrate some 183mm of armour at 550m and 172mm at 1,000m at a 30-degree angle. The accuracy of the APDS round was poor during World War II, however. By comparison, the standard M10's 3in M7 gun using APCBC ammunition could penetrate 97mm of armour at 550m at a 30-degree angle and 92mm of armour at 900m at a 30-degree angle. Only with HVAP ammunition did the M7 gun compare with the 17-pdr. US 3in HVAP ammunition was in very short supply, however, whereas the standard 17-pdr ammunition was available in quantity for the British Army.

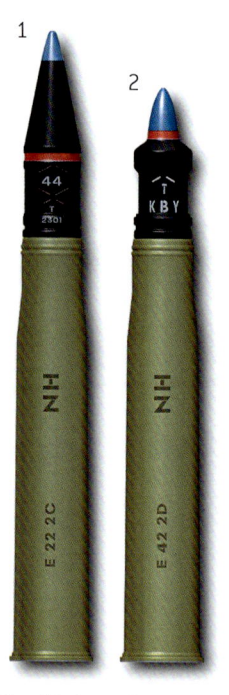

Four 17-pdr rounds used in the 17-pdr M10: Shot APCBC (**1**), Shot APDS (**2**), Shot Practice (**3**) and Shell HE (**4**).

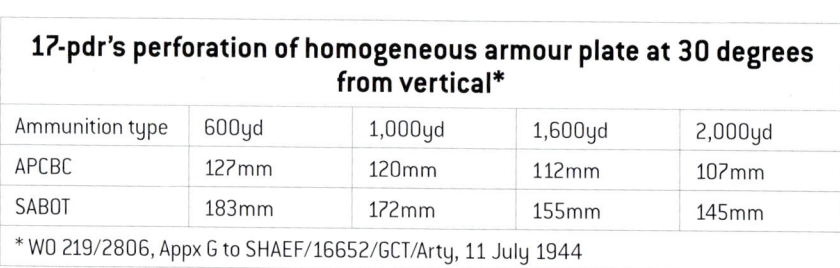

17-pdr's perforation of homogeneous armour plate at 30 degrees from vertical*				
Ammunition type	600yd	1,000yd	1,600yd	2,000yd
APCBC	127mm	120mm	112mm	107mm
SABOT	183mm	172mm	155mm	145mm
* WO 219/2806, Appx G to SHAEF/16652/GCT/Arty, 11 July 1944				

There were many factors affecting the performance of ammunition in battle, including variations in the armour quality of the target. From the practical soldier's point of view, 21st Army Group's firepower demonstration on 23 November 1944 using the gunners of 6 AT Regt RCA was probably good enough. One out of five hits using APCBC ammunition penetrated the frontal armour of a Panther tank hulk. Five out of nine hits with DS ammunition penetrated. This was a gun that could penetrate the toughest armour at typical engagement ranges in North-West Europe – maybe not every time, but it had a good chance of doing so.

The 17-pdr SP M10 was provided with an M51 direct-sighting telescope for direct fire, providing 3× magnification with a 13-degree field of view. Its US panoramic sight was replaced with a British dial sight and clinometer for indirect-fire artillery missions. Some units developed techniques for semi-indirect turret-down anti-tank shoots, claiming at least one kill using this approach. While the 17-pdr M10 was regularly used for indirect-fire missions, the Wehrmacht actively discouraged use of the Jagdpanther in this role for fear of excessive barrel wear and

17-pdr M10 TURRET

1. 17-pdr APDS Shot
2. 17-pdr APCBC Shot
3. Gunner's traverse handwheel
4. Gunner's M51 telescopic sight
5. Gun travel lock
6. QF 17-pdr Mk II in M5 mount
7. Folding brace for turret roof tarp
8. Sten machine carbine
9. Commander's seat
10. Loader's seat
11. Gunner's seat
12. .50in Browning machine gun

A close view of the 17-pdr breech, showing how cramped the Achilles turret was. There was even less turret space in the 17-pdr-armed Sherman Firefly tank. (Tank Museum 3000-A4)

to retain the element of surprise. The No. 1 of the 17-pdr M10 was equipped with a pair of binoculars, typically Mk 2 (Kelvin Prismatic) offering 6× magnification and an 8-degree field of view or Mk V (Ross Prismatic) with 7× magnification and a 7¾-degree field of view.

The 17-pdr M10 also mounted a .50-calibre M2 heavy machine gun for anti-aircraft defence on a pintle mount at the turret rear. This location was prompted by the desire to balance the weight of the turret, but it was not ideally placed for the M2's use against ground targets, because it could only be fired from inside the turret with the turret traversed to the rear. Otherwise, a crewman had to exit the turret and fire the M2 while standing exposed on the rear engine deck. Because the M10 was already out of production by the summer of 1944, there were no factory fixes to remedy the issue. Instead, some units in the field moved the M2 from the turret rear to a front location by welding a pintle mount onto one of the forward corners, despite the adverse effect this repositioning had on the balance of the turret.

Jagdpanther

The 8.8cm KwK 43 L/71 arming the Jagdpanther was among the most powerful anti-tank guns of World War II. It was designed to face the improved armour of Soviet tanks such as the JS series of heavy tanks. This was overkill for the Western Front, however, where most Allied armour could be penetrated at typical ranges. When used in conjunction with a stereoscopic rangefinder, Jagdpanther crews had the best chance of obtaining a first-round hit at long range.

At the beginning of July 1942, the German arms makers Krupp and Rheinmetall-Borsig were both invited to develop a new 8.8cm anti-tank gun. Rheinmetall-Borsig offered a version of their FlaK 41 L/74 anti-aircraft gun. Krupp designed an entirely new piece of ordnance, the KwK 43 L/71. This design was shorter than the FlaK 41

L/74, was fitted with a muzzle brake and used smaller projectiles. The Heereswaffenamt approved production of the KwK 43 L/71. This gun on a cruciform mounting was designated the 8.8cm PaK 43 in February 1943. The same ordnance mounted on the two-wheel carriage from the 10.5cm leFH 18 field howitzer was known as the 8.8cm PaK 43/41. The KwK 43 L/71 would also arm a series of AFVs including the Nashorn tank destroyer, the Jagdpanther and the PzKpfw VI Ausf B Tiger II/King Tiger heavy tank.

The PaK 43 was mounted in a central mantlet, with a traverse of 12 degrees to each side. The KwK 43 L/71 had originally been designed with a monobloc barrel but this was subsequently changed to a two-piece barrel to better withstand the high pressure generated when fired. It also made it easier to change the barrel, which needed to be replaced after 2,000 rounds, or as few as 1,200 when using the Pzgr 39-1 round. The two-piece barrel was fitted to Jagdpanthers built from May 1944 onwards. The gun could be dismounted by unbolting the mantlet and extracting the gun through the large hatch at the rear of the Jagdpanther's fighting compartment.

The Jagdpanther commander operated a Scherenfahrlafetten SF 14Z 'scissors' binocular telescope offering 10× magnification, which was superior in resolution to

A close-up of the later Jagdpanther variant's two-piece main-gun barrel. (Weald Foundation)

1   2

Four 8.8cm rounds used in the Jagdpanther: the Pzgr Patr 39/43, an APCBC-HE round (**1**); the Sprgr Patr 43, an HE round (**2**); the Gr Patr 39/43 HI, a shaped-charge round (**3**); and the Pzgr Patr 40/43, an APCR/HVAP round (**4**).

3   4

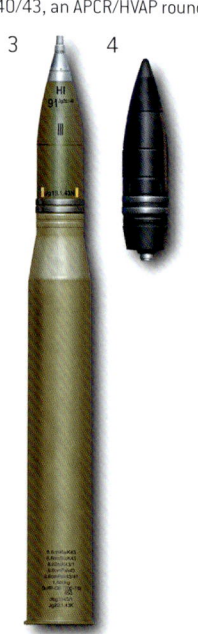

the binoculars available to Panzer commanders. The Jagdpanther's early sights, the Selbstfahrlafette-Zielfernrohr 1a (Sfl ZF 1a), were the same periscopes as those fitted on the Ferdinand/Elefant, but later vehicles used the Winkelzielfernrohr 1/4 (WZF 1/4) angled telescopic sight, as used by the towed PaK 43/41. The sight was linked with the main gun, eliminating the need for a large roof opening as used in *Sturmgeschütz* designs.

The radio-operator/hull machine-gunner, sitting in the front right-hand seat, operated the 7.92mm MG 34 machine gun housed in a ball mount on the right-hand side of the glacis plate. Its integrated 1.75× monocular sight provided an 18-degree field of view. In theory, the MG 34 fired 850rd/min from belts stored in 150-round canvas bags. A wooden box stored its sights, bipod mount, and wooden butt so the machine gun could be deployed out of the vehicle.

The Jagdpanther was issued with an Em 0,9 mR *Entfernungsmesser*, a stereoscopic rangefinder mounted on a tripod that could be deployed on the three mounting stubs located on the casemate roof. If operated by a trained operator with good stereoscopic vision, this rangefinder could provide an accurate range, helping to obtain a first-shot hit at long range.

For close-proximity defence, the Jagdpanther had a 9.2cm *Nahverteidigungswaffe*. This smoothbore breech-loading close-range grenade thrower was mounted at 50 degrees and could be rotated through 360 degrees, and was aimed using the periscopes on the casemate roof. It was compatible with the 2.3cm flare gun and could project a range of munitions, including *Schnellnebelkerzen* (smoke canisters), *Rauchsichtzeichen* (coloured-smoke canisters), *Leuchtgeschosse* (signal flares) and *Sprenggranatpatronen* (anti-personnel grenades).

The Jagdpanther had several advantages over the M10 in terms of fire control. Not only did the Jagdpanther have a gun sight that offered superior magnification, but it was also equipped with the stereoscopic rangefinder. The Jagdpanther's main gun was limited to a traverse of 11 degrees to either side of the centreline. This was not a critical disadvantage if the Jagdpanther was in an ambush position or at a long range from its target, but it became a significant risk at closer ranges.

JAGDPANTHER FIGHTING COMPARTMENT

1. 8.8cm PaK 43/3	6. Radio	11. Loader's seat	16. Driver's position
2. Mantlet	7. 8.8cm rounds	12. Drive shaft linkage	17. Periscope
3. Bow machine gun	8. Loader's seat	13. Gun foundation	
4. Radio operator's position	9. Breech	14. Gunner's seat	
5. Commander's position	10. Spent-round hole	15. Elevation wheel	

PROTECTION

There is no serious comparison between the protection characteristics of the M10 and Jagdpanther. While the M10 had very thin armour and had been designed to fulfil the role of a mobile tank destroyer, the Jagdpanther had frontal armour thick enough to defeat armour-piercing rounds fired from most tanks it was likely to meet on the battlefields of 1944–45.

The M10 was essentially an M4 medium tank fitted with thinner armour and a lightly armoured turret. Its frontal armour was only 60–75 per cent as thick as that of the M4, while the M10's side armour was more sloped. The M10's open turret rendered it vulnerable to mortars and artillery as well as overhead small-arms fire and grenades. It meant the No. 1 was forced to operate 'head up' and therefore with better vision and situational awareness than if operating closed down. Some anti-tank regiments created improvised roof armour for their vehicles. Some were of the opinion that the attitude of the No. 1 made the difference – a No. 1 who would operate with his head up would do so even if overhead cover was available; but the provision of overhead cover would not make any difference to those more cautious No. 1s who were reluctant to expose their heads.

Motivated by the unpleasant surprise of encountering the Red Army's fast and well-armoured T-34 medium tank, German designers were tasked with creating a copy of its Soviet adversary. The result was the Panther, with a low silhouette, a big gun on a

This frontal view of an Achilles shows the handle welded to the bolts intended to secure the additional armour plate. (Tank Museum 2999-F2)

turret mounted in the middle of the tank and armour distributed to provide heavy, strongly sloped, frontal armour and lightly armoured side and rear armour. The Jagdpanther, based on the Panther tank chassis, followed its model of protection.

The frontal upper armour of the Jagdpanther was a single steel plate, 80mm thick, angled at 55 degrees from vertical. This extended the frontal hull of the Panther design to the top of the casemate. The lower frontal armour, 60mm thick, was angled at 60 degrees. This resulted in an effective armour thickness of approximately 140mm RHAe for the upper plate and 90mm RHAe for the lower plate. The 100mm-thick *Saukopf* ('pig's head') gun mantlet was just as tough as the frontal armour. The sides of the superstructure had 50mm of armour, while the lower sides had 40mm. The roof and floor had armour of varying thickness, ranging from 16mm to 25mm. Overall, the Jagdpanther was a formidable AFV that, in principle, provided excellent protection to its five-man crew.

This apparently strong protection was undermined by some weaknesses in production, however. The armour had a tendency to fracture and give way if struck with armour-piercing projectiles. US metallurgical reports on frontal and side armour from Panther tanks identified the probable causes of these failures. The first issue, a shortage of molybdenum, resulted in the Germans replacing it with vanadium. The composition of armour tended to include 0.5 per cent carbon, 2 per cent chromium and 0.14 per cent vanadium. This relatively high carbon content was consistent with a poor shatter performance. The second issue was the quality of the process of quenching. If armour plates, particularly those over 40mm thick, were not quenched properly, invisible cracks could form, weakening the performance of the armour plates when hit. Furthermore, German substitutions in the composition of arc-welding electrodes were likely to have affected the quality of the welds. These faults may have been endemic in the drive for production quantity that characterized the German war industry in 1944.

The floor plates on the Jagdpanther were 16mm thick, with an additional 9mm beneath the driver and radio operator. Fitted to the hull sides, 5mm-thick *Schürzen*

plates were intended to diminish the effect of shaped-charge rounds against the running gear. The Jagdpanther's 100mm-thick *Topfblende* (pot mantlet) was a design that avoided creating a shot trap as per earlier models of the StuG III. It was a relatively soft, molybdenum-free steel casting bolted to the upper glacis for easier dismounting.

A three-quarter side view of a captured Jagdpanther hit by multiple projectiles. This is believed to be Major Sattler's vehicle, knocked out at Hechtel by 2 Welsh Guards (see pp. 63–64). (Imperial War Museums via Getty Images)

A view of the right side of the Jagdpanther, showing the gear stowed on the hull side above the armour skirts. (Weald Foundation)

MOBILITY

M10 Achilles

The M10c weighed 66,000lb with the 375bhp engine giving a power-to-weight ratio of around 11.5hp/ton. The M10, like the M4 on which it was based, had narrow tracks that were ill-suited to wet ground experienced in North-West Europe. Extended end-connecters offered better floating qualities on mud, but could catch on the hull overhang.

The General Motors 6/71 Diesel Model 6046 'twin six' engine was formed from two Detroit Diesel 6-71 inline engines mated to a single output. The tandem engine produced 375bhp (280kW) at 2,100rpm. One of the engines could be disconnected at will from the output and run independently so if one was knocked out or broke down, the other engine could be used to move the vehicle, albeit much more slowly. The M10A variant of the M10 was powered by the Ford GAA V-8 petrol engine, an eight-cylinder derivative of a V-12 aircraft engine project. It nominally delivered 500bhp (373kW) at 2,600rpm, but its actual performance was about 450bhp (336kW) at 2,600rpm, giving it comparable performance to the diesel version. The M10A was retained in the United States for training.

A tracked vehicle's basic mechanism of steering can be quite brutal, as it relies on one track slewing or skidding over the ground. Both the M10 and the Jagdpanther used a form of differential gearing that engaged a lower gear on one side than the other and produced a lower speed on one side than the other, which was less extreme than more primitive brake-and-clutch systems. The M10 shared its combined transmission, differential and final drives, called the 'Powertrain', with the M4 tank. The M10 had a turn radius of 26ft in first gear and 50ft in fifth. The Powertrain was robust and could tolerate abuse by heavy-handed driving in a manner that might break the more delicate Jagdpanther mechanism. For maintenance purposes, the M10's final drive could be accessed by unbolting the cover on the glacis plate.

The M10 had the vertical volute spring suspension (VVSS) of the M3 and M4 medium tanks. This was a robust system; it was easily maintained and units could be much more readily replaced and with much less labour than those of the Jagdpanther.

The armoured hull of the M10 was not watertight because it was not envisaged that the M10 would need to cross rivers in tactical settings, but it could and would be prepared for deep wading for amphibious operations such as the Normandy landings. Preparing the vehicle for wading watertight involved 253 man-hours of work, including sealing all the seams and welding extensions to the air intakes.

Jagdpanther

The Jagdpanther was powered by the 12-cylinder HL230 P30 V12 petrol engine, manufactured by

An Achilles ready to move. Regulations specified that when on the move, Achilles crews were to turn the turret to the six o'clock position, thereby allowing the main gun to rest on the rear clamp and placing the M2 machine gun facing towards the front of the vehicle. (Tank Museum 3000-A2)

Maybach, Auto Union and Daimler-Benz. This engine was also used in the Panther and later models of the Tiger I tank. The Jagdpanther's 23.88-litre engine was rated at 510kW (684bhp) at 3,000rpm but realistically delivered around 485kW (650bhp) at 2,500rpm. This was a very powerful tank engine for the era, delivering much more power than the engines used to power British, Soviet and US tanks. Fans protected by mesh and a grating on each side of the engine forced air-cooling air out. The cyclone action of the air around the holes helped to filter out larger dirt and dust particles that fell out of the filter box. The use of dry air filters was an innovation for German tanks, which had previously used 'wet' (oil-based) air filters.

The engine's power was transferred to the running gear by the ZF (Zahnradfabrik Friedrichshafen) AK 7-200 transmission, specially developed for the Panther by ZF and later replaced by a strengthened ZF AK 7-400 transmission. During the transmission's development process, ZF came up with a new concept. Between February and August 1942, the company created the AK 7-200 seven-speed manual transmission. This was based on lorry transmissions of that time and was relatively compact. It also had a cost-effective cone synchronizer, to transition smoothly between gears that rotated at different speeds. Only first and reverse gear were unsynchronized.

The weak point in the Jagdpanther's transmission was the final drive, which had a life far lower than that of the engine. The root cause of the problem was the decision to use two spur gear sets rather than an epicyclic gear system for the final reduction of the driving rpm – a risky choice as the steel available at that stage of the war did not have a high stress tolerance. An epicyclic gear system had been tested successfully as a prototype, but a shortage of suitable gear-cutting machinery precluded its use in production vehicles. If the steering or brakes were handled roughly, momentum could build up causing breaks in the gear teeth or the undersized transmission shaft (Spielberger 2004: 56–60). In particular, the final drives were prone to failure when the Jagdpanther steered in reverse when operating on rough ground (Jentz 2004: 141–42). In September–October 1944, a series of modifications were incorporated into the final drives to counter reported problems including chewed-up gear teeth, broken parts, damaged bearings and insufficient lubrication (Jentz 2004: 96).

The Jagdpanther had a MAN (Maschinenfabrik Augsburg-Nürnberg) single-radius controlled differential, steering levers, mechanical disc brakes and a turn radius that varied from 5m (16ft) in first gear to 43m (141ft) in fifth gear. The driver made the turn by selecting the gear with the right ratio. The Jagdpanther's transmission was not easily accessible, however, and required the removal of the main armament and the mantlet, as well as the driver's and wireless operator's seats.

While the Jagdpanther was lower, cheaper and quicker to manufacture than the Panther, it was marginally heavier and its speed marginally worse, as well as being nose-heavy. The power-to-weight ratio of about 8hp/ton was less than ideal for an AFV, so the Germans employed some clever engineering to create a suspension that could provide mobility over rough or muddy terrain.

The Jagdpanther utilized the Schachtellaufwerk suspension format, designed by Professor Ernst Lauf and widely used in German half-tracks. It featured large, overlapping, interleaved road wheels with a 'slack-track' using no return rollers for the upper run of the track. This system combined wide travel stroke and rapid oscillations with high reliability to allow relatively high-speed travel over difficult terrain (Spielberger 2004: 60–68).

The Jagdpanther had 16 plate-shaped rubber-rimmed road wheels 86cm (35in) in diameter on each side, which were arranged as eight nested double road wheels, four in pairs with the 'deep' sides facing outwards and four in pairs with the 'deep' sides facing inwards at the ends the wheel hubs were attached. The inner rollers had a locking ring that was designed as a contact ring against the chain guide teeth.

A double torsion-bar suspension with swing arms provided independent wheel movement in the vertical and increased stiffness in turns, which helped to maintain stability over rough terrain. The torsion bar crossed the hull and attached to a pivot inside the hull, which attached to a second torsion bar that crossed back over to be anchored against the hull on the same side as the wheel it was attached to. The Jagdpanther also had a 17-tooth front drive sprocket, an adjustable rear idler, one return roller per track, and shock absorbers on the second and seventh road wheels. The multiple large, rubber-rimmed steel wheels distributed ground pressure more evenly across the track, making the vehicle more stable when moving across rough ground. According to US accounts, this made the Jagdpanther capable of crossing terrain that would defeat the M4 and its derivatives, such as the M10.

The suspension design had some disadvantages, however, and was not copied in post-war AFV designs. The suspension and track could become clogged with mud, ice and snow, and the design complicated maintenance and repairs to road wheels and torsion bars, requiring the removal of four or five other wheels to work on any one road wheel. Additionally, the configuration of the Jagdpanther stressed the suspension further. If driven carelessly, travel at speed over rough ground could result in the suspension hitting the bump stops. In contrast, the M10's VVSS suspension was robust, easily maintained and offered easier replacement of units with much less labour than those of the Jagdpanther.

The Jagdpanther's hull was watertight to allow for wading. The side-effect of this was that fuel and oil from engine leaks would not drain away but collect in the bottom of the hull, adding to the fire risk.

ABOVE LEFT
The front of the Jagdpanther's right-side running gear is revealed by the absence of the front part of the armour skirts. (Weald Foundation)

ABOVE RIGHT
A view of the rear of the Jagdpanther's right-side running gear. Note the spare track links carried above the rail for the armour skirts. (Weald Foundation)

STRATEGIC MOBILITY

Strategic mobility – the ability of an AFV to move distances to the battle area or in major moves in advance, pursuit or withdrawal – is a function of weight and size as well as long-distance on-road performance. The weight of an AFV determines the bridges and roads it can use and the cranes and road and rail transporters that can carry it. Rail was a key means of strategic transport during World War II. The rail gauge constrained the railway routes that could be used, however, as out-of-gauge loads might strike bridges or tunnels. In these terms, the smaller, lighter and far more reliable M10 had strategic mobility far superior to that of the Jagdpanther. Put simply, there were far more Class 30-ton bridges and roads than Class 45-ton.

Geography had a major influence on transport. US-built AFVs needed to be transported overseas and the M10 could be loaded using the same dock cranes and took up no more space on a ship than an M4 tank. It would have caused enormous logistic problems in the United States to field an AFV the size and weight of the Jagdpanther.

The M10's superior reliability was an important factor in strategic road moves. The Panther had been hurriedly put into production before its teething problems had been resolved and had been plagued by engine fires, engine and transmission failures. These had not been resolved by the time the Jagdpanther entered combat. Typically, M4-derived AFVs had around a 1 per cent breakdown rate on road moves, compared to 10–20 per cent for late-war German types based on the Tiger I or Panther tanks. The Jagdpanther was not capable of completing strategic moves without a high number of breakdowns. The initial deployment of schwere Panzerjäger-Abteilung 654 involved about 25 Jagdpanthers undertaking a 300km (186 miles) road march from the rail head at Rocquigny, near the Belgian border. During the journey, the 27

A 17-pdr Achilles of 93 AT Regt RA crosses the Savio River via a Churchill ARK near Cesena, Italy, 24 October 1944. A second Achilles can be discerned in the background. Note the partly submerged Panther medium tank at left. (Tank Museum 3000-D2)

vehicles incurred damage to 18 final drives, two engines, two oil coolers, three cooling fans, one torsion bar, four road wheels, one drive shaft, four drive sprockets, two idler wheels and 109 track links. Not surprisingly, Germany relied first and foremost on rail transport to move its tanks and tank destroyers to the battle area.

This vision slit is immediately to the right of the Jagdpanther's main gun. (Weald Foundation)

COMMAND AND CONTROL

Both the Jagdpanther and the 17-pdr M10 were fitted with radios for communication among the vehicles within sub-units as well as to provide connections with higher headquarters.

The 17-pdr M10 was fitted with the British No. 19 set, developed by the Signals Experimental Detachment and Pye Radio for use in tanks and armoured vehicles, in place of the US Army's SCR-610 set initially fitted to the M10. The No. 19 set consisted of four elements: an 'A' set, operating on 2–8MHz and used for communications with base or other troops at ranges up to 10 miles; a 'B' set, operating on 230–240MHz and used for communication between vehicles in a troop at ranges up to 1,000yd; an Inter Communication (IC) amplifier, for speech between the crew; and a supply unit. The No. 19 set was tuned to receive and transmit with a single dial and had a 'flick' switch for rapidly changing between two frequencies.

The standard radio fit in the Jagdpanther was the FuG 5, a 10-watt USW transceiver. The Jagdpanthers of platoon leaders and higher commanders had the expanded FuG 15 set, which added a receiver to monitor a broader range of communication networks. German radios were of good quality, but AM radios had inherent limitations when used from moving vehicles.

The roof of the Jagdpanther's fighting compartment had two circular hatches. The two projections above the left hatch are to locate the base of the stereoscopic rangefinder. The operator would need to be exposed to use this equipment, which may not have been a problem if the engagement occurred at the 2.5km range specified in the manual. (Weald Foundation)

THE COMBATANTS

During World War II there was an important factor that differentiated self-propelled anti-tank guns from tanks. The former were not designed to be operated by the armoured arm, but by an anti-tank arm, whether it was the US Army's Tank Destroyer Command, the British Army's Royal Regiment of Artillery or the Wehrmacht's *Panzerjäger*. Each of these arms of service had a distinctive ethos and doctrine that influenced AFV development and use.

A 17-pdr Achilles crew enjoy a tea break, their vehicle partly covered by a tarpaulin. (Tank Museum 4389-E1)

BRITISH AND CANADIAN ANTI-TANK ORGANIZATION

The British Army entered World War II with insufficient anti-tank weapons, a problem exacerbated by the losses incurred during 1940. One lesson learned by British forces during the 1940 campaign was the need for increased numbers of anti-tank units. Dozens of additional anti-tank units were formed in 1941–42, with an anti-tank regiment per division and corps.

By 1944 there was a division of responsibilities between the different types of units equipped with anti-tank guns. British anti-tank guns were organized at battalion, division and corps level. Each infantry battalion included an anti-tank platoon of six 6-pdr anti-tank guns crewed by infantrymen, supplemented by an allocation of the PIAT (Projector Infantry Anti-Tank), a hand-held, close-range weapon comparable to the German *Panzerfaust*.

Each infantry division had a Royal Artillery anti-tank regiment of four batteries, each with four 12-gun batteries. Each battery was equipped with a mixture of towed 6-pdr and 17-pdr anti-tank guns, towed by field-artillery tractors and Universal Carriers respectively. The three D-Day assault divisions – 3rd British, 3rd Canadian and 50th (Northumbrian) – received 3in M10s in lieu of towed 17-pdrs. During the winter of 1944/45, a proportion of the towed 17-pdrs were replaced with the 17-pdr Valentine self-propelled gun known as the Archer.

Each armoured division and army corps included an anti-tank regiment of 48 guns organized into four batteries. Each battery had three troops, each commanded by a lieutenant and fielding four guns. Two batteries were each equipped with 12 towed 17-pdr guns with Crusader or Ram tracked or M14 semi-tracked gun tractors. The other two batteries were equipped with M10s. The proportion of 17-pdr-armed M10s increased during the campaign in North-West Europe.

BRITISH AND CANADIAN ANTI-TANK TACTICS AND TRAINING

British and Canadian anti-tank unit tactics emphasized surprise action from well-concealed positions at effective range. In defence, guns were to be sited to cover likely armoured approaches in depth. In an attack on any ground suitable for armour, attacking troops would be liable to an immediate counter-attack by tanks. Attacks were to be supported by anti-tank guns pushed forward.

Each infantry battalion's 6-pdrs would be sited to protect the battalion, while an infantry division's anti-tank regiment would be deployed in killing areas based on likely enemy armoured approaches. Corps-level anti-tank regiments were to provide mobile detachments of powerful anti-tank weapons that could be used to strengthen defences, or in the case of M10s, support offensives on any part of the corps' front. Unlike

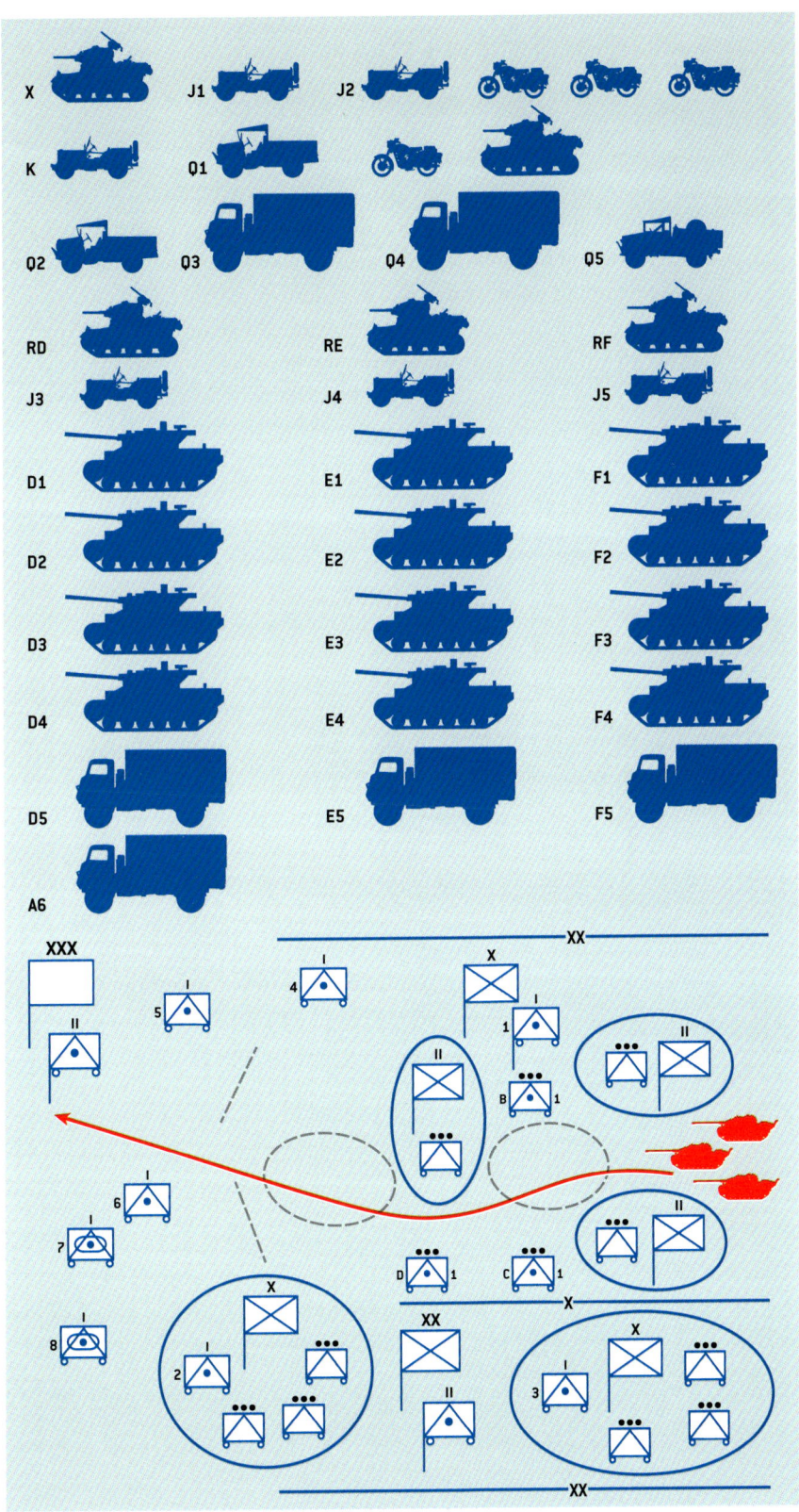

The upper part of this diagram depicts the organization of a Canadian anti-tank battery. The battery commander (**X**) is equipped with an M5 light tank. His recce group included two battery officers (**J1** and **J2**) plus the battery sergeant major and two orderlies. The vehicle used by the second-in-command, the battery captain, was marked **K**; here, he also has an M5 light tank. His party included a cook (**Q1**) and the battery clerk (**Q2**). Each of the three troops had a troop commander (**RD**, **RE** and **RF**), a troop sergeant (**J3**, **J4** and **J5**) and four 17-pdr SP M10 guns (**D1–D4**, **E1–E4** and **F1–F4**). The transport group included the battery quartermaster sergeant and his vehicles (**Q3–Q5**) plus the three troops' ammunition vehicles (**D5**, **E5** and **F5**) and the gun fitter (**A6**). Below is a schematic layout of anti-tank defences for a British or Canadian infantry division with three infantry brigades, the divisional anti-tank regiment and the corps anti-tank regiment. Each infantry battalion (three per brigade) had an anti-tank platoon with six 6-pdr guns for self-defence. The divisional anti-tank regiment's four batteries (numbered 1–4) each had two troops with four towed 17-pdrs and one with four 6-pdrs, sited to cover killing areas (indicated with grey dashed lines). The corps anti-tank regiment's two towed batteries (5 and 6), each with 12 17-pdrs, formed a backstop to the defences, while the two batteries equipped with the 17-pdr M10 SP (7 and 8) provided the reserve. This gave the divisional commander 70 6-pdrs and 32 towed 17-pdrs, backed by 24 towed and 24 self-propelled 17-pdrs at corps level.

armour, in which the troop commander commanded his troop from a tank, the anti-tank troop commander led on foot or from a separate vehicle, nominally an armoured OP Universal Carrier. The battery commander was also issued a Universal Carrier.

Taking a broader view, British and Canadian fighting methods in Normandy have been described as an updated version of the World War I tactics of 'Bite and Hold'. After seizing a tactically significant piece of ground under a heavy artillery barrage, British infantry and armour would then prepare this ground for defence against the inevitable counter-attack that was part of German doctrine. Allied field artillery would pummel the counter-attacking infantrymen, but anti-tank guns would be needed to deal with supporting German armour. The 6-pdr guns organic to British infantry battalions and Royal Artillery anti-tank regiments were adequate to see off PzKpfw IV medium tanks and *Sturmgeschütz* assault guns, but 17-pdrs were needed to tackle Panther medium or Tiger heavy tanks. The huge towed 17-pdr gun was so large that it took around 12 hours to dig it in. As a consequence, 17-pdr M10s were in constant demand to accompany attacks and provide anti-tank protection until Allied defences could be prepared fully.

The training necessary to put these tactics into practice was broadly similar across the British and Canadian armies. The first six weeks or so of military life were given over to learning arms and foot drill as a method for imbuing recruits with military discipline. By mid-war this period was also used to sort soldiers into appropriate specialisms. The partially trained recruits were assigned one of three trades.

Gunners undertook an eight-week course, learning the duties of every gun number, although they would not be expected to serve as a No. 1 after eight weeks. The ultimate aim was speed, but the emphasis was on correct drills and accurate laying. The course would have been based on the 2-pdr gun drill, later replaced with that of the 6-pdr. The only topics not taught were zeroing, examining equipment, disablement and dismantling of equipment.

The aim of the 12-week driver-training course was to produce drivers capable of maintaining their vehicle and driving under all conditions. As well as elementary gun towing, drivers were taught enough gunnery to be able to replace gun-crew casualties, handle ammunition and recognize Allied and enemy AFVs. Drivers were taught to drive cars, trucks and 30cwt portees. After only 60 hours the driver was not expected to have developed full road sense. Motorcycle dispatch riders had a separate course.

The third anti-tank trade was signaller. This training lasted 18 weeks and aimed to produce a regimental signaller capable of operating all communications equipment except visual (semaphore and heliograph). Trainee signallers were taught enough gunnery to be able to replace gun-crew casualties or act as look-outs.

While the duties of signallers and drivers in an anti-tank regiment might have been familiar to those from field-artillery or anti-aircraft-artillery units, gunners had to be trained on the new equipment. Officers needed to learn how to deploy and command their troops. The unit would need to learn how to move and fight as a team. Much training with the 6-pdr would have involved manhandling the gun. The British and Canadian military ethos included the use of competitive sports to develop team spirit, with inter-troop and battery baseball and hockey featuring in recreational activities.

The tactics learned and employed by the anti-tank regiments had to evolve as their equipment changed. The anti-tank regiment serving in British VIII Corps, 91 AT Regt RA, was originally converted from 5th Battalion, The Argyll and Sutherland

Highlanders, in November 1941. The regimental history records a similar progression from 2-pdr to 6-pdr then 17-pdr and M10, receiving the last of its 17-pdr M10s a few days before deploying across the Channel in mid-1944. The historian Desmond Flower noted (1950) that while the soldiers of 91 AT Regt RA were well trained in gunnery and deployment drills, the regiment had little idea about the M10's tactical capabilities; nor was there tactical training with the other arms.

6 ANTI-TANK REGIMENT RCA

The announcement of the formation of First Canadian Army's two army corps (I and II) necessitated the formation of two anti-tank regiments, one per corps. In April 1942, 6 AT Regt RCA was formed in Petawawa, Ontario, from 33, 56, 74 and 103 batteries. It was originally intended to be part of 6th Canadian Infantry Division and deployed on the Pacific Coast in a Home Service role, with many soldiers recruited for home service only. The batteries were initially understrength and numbers were made up with men from the training depots. It would have taken several months for the regiment's commanding officer, Lieutenant-Colonel J.A. Blackey, to have welded this body of soldiers into a regiment.

In January 1943, the regiment received the news that it was to serve overseas. At the end of May, its 6-pdr anti-tank guns were loaded in crates and dispatched to Britain and the regiment departed by train for Debert, Nova Scotia, where the troops passed the time with route marches and as much recreation as possible while waiting to embark. Once in England, the regiment was based at Marden Park near Caterham, Surrey, coming under command of II Canadian Corps. At the end of November 1943, the regiment went into billets at Seaford, Sussex, under a new CO, Lieutenant-Colonel L.A. Devine, formerly CO 7 AT Regt, I Canadian Corps' anti-tank regiment.

CHARLES KYDD

Charles Hewson Kydd was born on 23 May 1912 in Portland, Oregon, but was educated in Truro, Nova Scotia. He joined the Canadian Bank of Commerce in 1931 and worked in various branches until he enlisted in the military in 1941.

Kydd was sent to England in November 1941, joining 7 AT Regt RCA on 12 June 1942, in which he served as a troop commander in 111 Bty. Based in Sussex, his unit trained as part of the Home Forces, initially to face a German invasion and then for active service overseas. The unit was equipped with towed 6-pdr and 17-pdr anti-tank guns. While in 111 Bty, Kydd picked up the nickname 'Capie'. He left 7 AT Regt RCA on 11 June 1943 to return to Canada as an instructor at the artillery training centres at Petawawa, Ontario, until he was deployed overseas again in 1944.

Initially posted to a reinforcement regiment, Kydd joined 6 AT Regt RCA on 7 September 1944, as one of the replacements for officer casualties during the fighting in Normandy. He was the new boy joining an experienced team. Although he had served as a gunnery instructor, he was joining a unit that had proved itself in battle during the Normandy campaign. When he joined the regiment, it was taking part in the pursuit from the Seine River and his initial appointment was as the operations officer in regimental headquarters. At this time, 6 AT Regt RCA was four junior officers understrength and by 14 October Kydd was a troop commander in 56 Bty in command of four M10s and their crews. The battery he joined had taken part in the battles between Caen and Falaise, the closure of the Falaise Gap and the capture of Boulogne and Calais, where the M10s were used as assault guns. One of the Calais forts fell to E Troop, which took four German officers and 250 men prisoner.

The October 1944–January 1945 period was a relatively uneventful time as II Canadian Corps took over a quiet sector

Charles Hewson Kydd. (CIBC Archives)

of the Netherlands–Germany border. This gave Kydd an opportunity to get to know the soldiers of Easy Troop and prove his competence. On 26 February, two weeks after the action for which he was awarded the Military Cross, Kydd was wounded when his M5 light tank ran over a mine and was subjected to shell and mortar fire. He was evacuated to hospital. Kydd was released from active service in February 1946 and returned to work for the Canadian Bank of Commerce at the Montague branch in Prince Edward Island, Canada. He died on 26 February 1996 in Halifax, Nova Scotia.

Over the winter of 1943/44, the regiment received new equipment: 33 and 56 batteries were re-equipped with M10s while 74 and 103 batteries received 17-pdr guns towed by Canadian Ram tanks, though it would be May 1944 before all the towers arrived. The conversion to self-propelled equipment and tracked gun tractors required extensive training for drivers and an enhancement to the maintenance capability. While there might have been training in the technical aspects of gunnery, there may have been limited opportunities for training with other arms. In April 1944, the regiment relocated to II Canadian Corps' concentration area near Hythe, Kent, prior to the move across the Channel.

GERMAN ANTI-TANK ORGANIZATION

The initial organization of a *schwere Panzerjäger-Abteilung (Panther)* called for a *Stab*, or headquarters, with three Jagdpanthers and a *Stabskompanie* with signals, armoured-engineer and anti-aircraft-artillery platoons under command. Oberleutnant Franz Kopka, who served as a company commander with schwere Panzerjäger-Abteilung 559, also mentions a medical platoon in his post-war account of the battalion's history, but it is unlikely that all battalions had their full complement of these support units. The battalion was to contain three fighting companies, each equipped with 14 Jagdpanthers. In early September 1944, a new organization was introduced whereby only one company was to be equipped with Jagdpanthers while the second and third companies were outfitted with Sturmgeschütz III assault guns and later with Jagdpanzer IV tank destroyers.

GERMAN ANTI-TANK TACTICS AND TRAINING

Captured and translated German training and tactical manuals give some insights into the performance and handling of the Jagdpanther in battle. It was noted that it could destroy all known types of enemy tanks at long ranges, with 2,500m being considered a practical range for engaging enemy vehicles. As well as its long-range role, the Jagdpanther's cross-country performance and armour protection enabled it to assist friendly tanks in frontal attacks, but its limited traverse, vision, and available means of defence at close quarters meant that it could not be used in the tank role and made it necessary for it to be protected by infantry or tanks.

Strong emphasis was placed on the Jagdpanther-equipped unit being deployed as a battalion whenever possible. According to doctrine, single companies could be placed under corps or divisional command, but not lower. The Jagdpanther unit commander was to be consulted before tasks were allotted to his vehicles. In all circumstances he remained responsible for the execution of his task and the repair of his vehicles. The employment of individual sections (four Jagdpanthers each) was only permissible when attacking fortified positions or when operating in close country. The use of Jagdpanthers on an individual basis was forbidden.

The manual notes that Jagdpanthers should be positioned where the enemy's main effort was located, in support of friendly anti-tank units. Commanders were reminded that the Jagdpanther was not a static anti-tank gun, nor an artillery piece on a self-propelled carriage. The Jagdpanthers' use of high-explosive ammunition on unarmoured targets was only permissible if no enemy tanks were present and if there were no other heavy guns available or if they had been knocked out – and then only if the ammunition supply permitted.

Commanders were told that full use had to be made of the range of the Jagdpanther's 8.8cm gun when attacking enemy tanks, particularly when the enemy enjoyed a large numerical superiority. When Jagdpanthers were in concealed positions unknown to the enemy, they were to let enemy tanks move into their field of fire and engage them

A Jagdpanther crewman stands by his vehicle, France, mid-1944. (Bundesarchiv, Bild 1011-721-0396-24/Wagner/ CC BY-SA 3.0 de)

A view of the left rear corner of a Jagdpanther's fighting compartment. Already severely corroded, the interior of this vehicle has been stripped of its ammunition. (Tank Museum 0876-B6)

at short range using the element of surprise. Concentration of fire was desirable. When engaging targets, full use was to be made of manoeuvrability, with firing positions changed frequently. Crews were reminded that enemy tank attacks could be pinned down by a proportion of Jagdpanthers, while the rest attacked the enemy tanks from the flank or rear and destroyed them.

During an attack by friendly tanks, the tasks of a Jagdpanther unit included: support of the first wave by engaging enemy medium and heavy tanks; pinning down the enemy tanks from the front while the enemy flanks or rear were being attacked; and the protection of one or both flanks of the attacking tanks. In the case of an attack by infantry, Jagdpanthers were to follow immediately behind the leading riflemen. Their main task was then to engage enemy tanks to the front and to the flanks. If no enemy tanks were present, Jagdpanthers could use high-explosive ammunition or machine-gun fire to assist the infantry attack.

After completing their mission at the front, Jagdpanthers were to be withdrawn for repair and maintenance, in order to ensure that the unit remained ready for action.

SCHWERE PANZERJÄGER-ABTEILUNG 655

On 15 April 1943, schwere Panzerjäger-Abteilung 655 was raised as headquarters for Panzerjäger-Kompanien 521, 611 and 670. These companies were re-formed with the same numbers as *Panzerjäger* battalions destroyed during the battle of Stalingrad in 1942–43. The core of the battalion may have included veterans from these three companies who were not present in Stalingrad at the time of the German surrender. The companies had served as independent *Panzerjäger* units equipped with towed and self-propelled equipment since operations in the West during 1940.

The battalion was initially equipped with Nashorn tank destroyers. On 1 September 1943, schwere Panzerjäger-Abteilung 655 with 40 Nashorns was assigned to

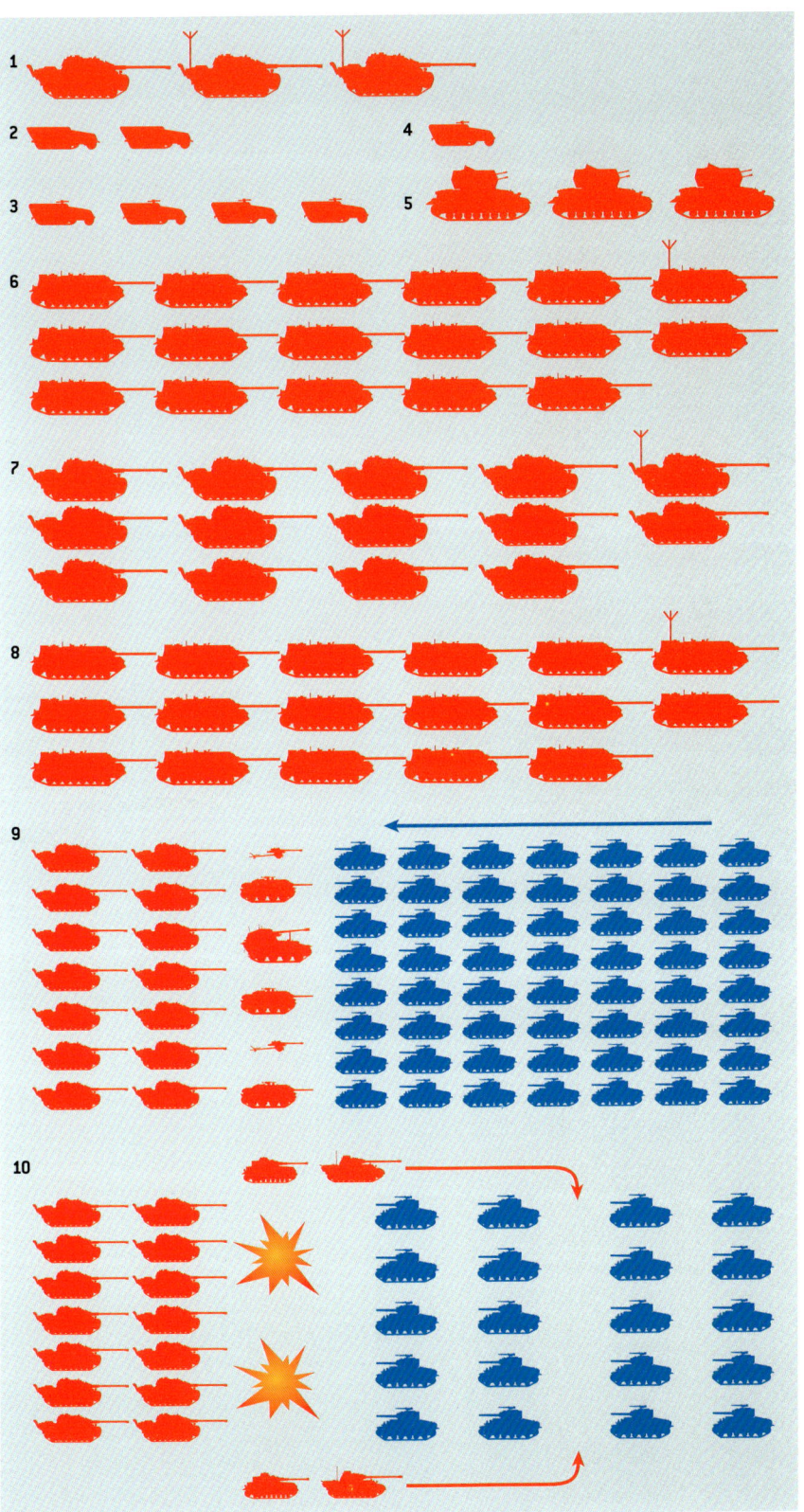

These diagrams depict the organization of a *schwere Panzerjäger-Abteilung* (**1–8**) above two tactical scenarios involving Jagdpanthers, one in defence (**9**) and the other in the attack (**10**). The battalion headquarters (**1**) had three Jagdpanthers, while the medical platoon (**2**) had two half-tracks and the engineer platoon (**3**) had four and the signals platoon (**4**) had one; the anti-aircraft platoon (**5**) had three Flakpanzer IVs. Here, the 1st and 3rd companies (**6** and **8**) are equipped with the 7.5cm-armed Panzer IV/70(V), while the 2nd company (**7**) has the Jagdpanther. German tactical instructions for the Jagdpanther emphasized that the unit should be used as a battalion, occasionally in detached companies, and only as platoons against fortifications; the use of individual Jagdpanthers was forbidden. In defence (**9**), the Jagdpanther was to be deployed in complete units against the enemy's point of main effort, reinforcing existing anti-tank weapons. The Jagdpanthers should exploit the range of their armament engage enemy armour from 2,700m (2,952yd). In the attack (**10**), Jagdpanthers were to pick off heavy and medium tanks while other friendly armour manoeuvred around the enemy's flanks. Jagdpanthers were not considered to be static guns and were not to be deployed to defend a position. Their crews were instructed to change position frequently and engage the foe from unexpected angles. After combat Jagdpanthers were to be withdrawn for maintenance.

A view of the ceiling of a Jagdpanther's fighting compartment, looking towards the upper front right corner. (Tank Museum 0876-C3)

XXVII. Armeekorps in Heeresgruppe Mitte, in which it took part in the defence against the Soviet autumn offensive. On 1 October 1943, the unit transferred to XXXIX. Panzerkorps. On 2 April 1944, the three companies were redesignated '1', '2' and '3' before participating in the fighting during the Red Army's Operation *Bagration*, the Soviet summer offensive launched on 22 June 1944.

The battalion's soldiers were recruited from East and West Prussia (modern-day Poland and Russian Kaliningrad). While many would have been new recruits to make up for the men lost in the fighting of 1943–44, a significant number would have been veterans. Some of the newer recruits may have been assigned to work in the plants manufacturing the Jagdpanther as there were severe labour shortages in the armaments

French refugees pass two destroyed Marder III Ausf M self-propelled tank destroyers of Panzerjäger-Abteilung 243, Roncey, 6 August 1944. The 7.5cm PaK 40 anti-tank gun armed these open-topped vehicles based on the Czechoslovak PzKpfw 38(t) light tank. (Fred Ramage/Keystone/Hulton Archive/Getty Images)

HERMANN FELDHEIM

Born in Buchholz, Harburg, on 30 September 1919, Hermann Feldheim joined Panzerjäger-Abteilung 20 in June 1940 as a detachment commander. He served as a platoon commander in Operation *Barbarossa* during summer 1941 and was awarded the EK 2 on 4 October. Feldheim was promoted to *Leutnant der Reserve* on 1 November and transferred to a training and replacement unit, joining schwere Panzerjäger-Abteilung 654 in April 1943. Credited with destroying 16 Soviet tanks during the battle of Kursk and wounded in the action, he was awarded the EK 1 and *Panzerkampfabzeichen* in July 1943. He remained with 1./sPzJgAbt 654 throughout 1944, joining the battle in Normandy in August 1944; his company's Jagdpanthers were unable to find a crossing point over the Seine River and were lost. Wounded again in December 1944, Feldheim continued to serve with the unit in Alsace with sufficient distinction to be awarded the *Deutsches Kreuz in Gold* in January 1945.

Oberleutnant Hermann Feldheim, the Jagdpanther commander who knocked out most of a squadron of Churchill tanks on 31 July 1944. (Bundesarchiv, Bild 101I-721-0397-12/Wagner/CC BY-SA 3.0 de)

FRIEDRICH LÜDERS

Friedrich Lüders was born on 19 May 1918. He was awarded the EK 1 and EK 2 during World War II. On 12 February 1943, he was awarded the *Deutsches Kreuz in Gold*; at this time he was an *Oberleutnant* in 2./PzJgAbt 654, at that time equipped with a mixture of self-propelled 7.5cm Marder II and towed PaK 40 anti-tank guns during the defensive fighting of winter 1942/43. Lüders was promoted to *Hauptmann* and commanded 2./sPzJgAbt 654 during the Normandy campaign. In September 1944 he was awarded the *Ritterkreuz*. He survived the war, and died on 15 May 1993.

industry. Interrogation of prisoners taken in the Reichswald fighting noted that the morale within schwere Panzerjäger-Abteilung 655 seemed to be high, despite soldiers being aware that Germany was losing the war.

On 13 September 1944, schwere Panzerjäger-Abteilung 655 was reorganized into two assault-gun companies (1. and 3.) and one Jagdpanther company (2.) after being deployed on the Eastern Front. About the third week of December, after a period of training in the East, the unit was transferred in stages via Berlin and Hannover to the training area near Paderborn, where it was brought up to strength with 45 *Panzerjäger*. It was deployed to Speyer on the west bank of the Rhine south of Mannheim, prior to commitment to combat. While there the unit's vehicles were painted white for snow camouflage. Less than a week later there was a revision of plans. Between 18 and 22 January 1945, schwere Panzerjäger-Abteilung 655 started to move north on a frequently interrupted and roundabout route via Wesel to the Geldern area. Here the unit detrained about the beginning of February, making final preparations before being committed in combat. The white colour on the unit's vehicles was washed off.

THE STRATEGIC SITUATION

The cross-Channel assault envisaged by Allied planners in 1944 was based on some assumptions. They expected their forces to be faced by the full might of Germany's Wehrmacht in the West. Operation *Overlord*, the battle for Normandy, was mounted by an advance force of 30 divisions to seize a lodgement with deep-water ports into which the bulk of the US forces could deploy direct to the Continent. The landscape of the Normandy battlefield could be divided into two. The country to the west of Bayeux, the US sector, was *bocage*, characterized by substantial hedgerows and small fields. It was

Photographed in 2017, this Jagdpanther is displayed at the Patriot Museum Complex, Kubinka, Russia. (Alan Wilson/ Wikimedia/CC BY-SA 2.0)

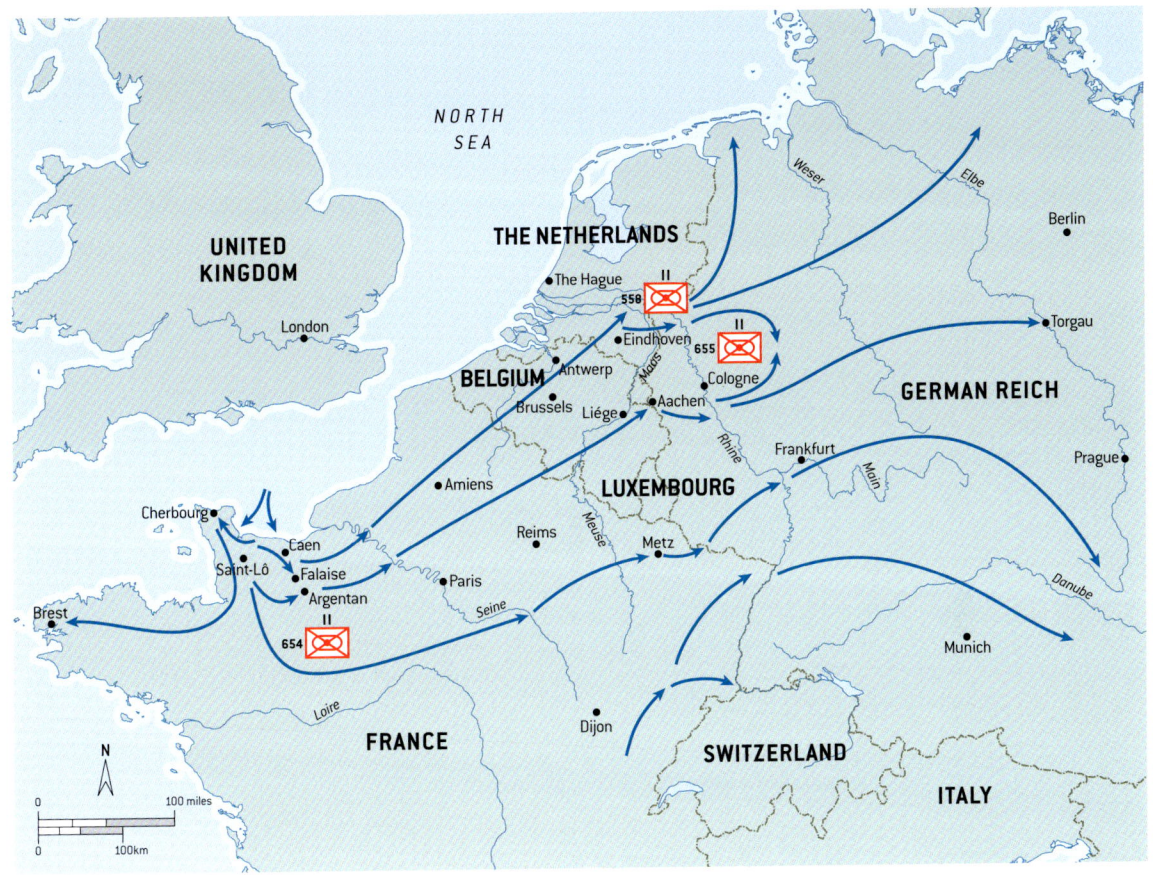

NORTH SEA

UNITED KINGDOM

London

THE NETHERLANDS

The Hague

Eindhoven

Antwerp

BELGIUM

Brussels

Liége

Aachen

Cologne

GERMAN REICH

Berlin

Torgau

Weser

Elbe

Maas

Rhine

Frankfurt

Prague

Main

LUXEMBOURG

Amiens

Reims

Meuse

Metz

Munich

Danube

Cherbourg

Caen

Saint-Lô

Falaise

Argentan

Paris

Seine

Brest

Loire

Dijon

FRANCE

SWITZERLAND

ITALY

558

655

654

N

0   100 miles

0   100km

This map shows the lines of advance of the British and Canadian forces in North-West Europe during 1944–45 and the locations of three Jagdpanther-equipped German anti-tank battalions that fought them (sPzJgAbt 654 in July–August 1944, during Operation *Bluecoat*; sPzJgAbt 558 in September 1944, during Operation *Market Garden*; and sPzJgAbt 655 in February 1945, during Operation *Veritable*).

poor tank country, which would serve to protect the Allied beachhead from German armoured attacks. The eastern half, from Bayeux to Caen, was much more open, offering better going for tanks; this was the area into which the Germans might be expected to launch their armour en masse. The British and Canadian troops scheduled to land here might be expected to face perhaps 200 German tanks within hours of coming ashore – and many of these could be Tigers or Panthers. The Allies faced the prospect of possibly having to fight a big tank battle from the Channel surf itself.

Accordingly, British and Canadian anti-tank units in the initial invasion force were expected to play a major part in operations on D-Day and thereafter. The anti-tank regiments of the three assault divisions were equipped with a mix of towed 6-pdr guns and 3in M10s rather than towed 17-pdr guns. The two corps anti-tank regiments, 62 (British I Corps) and 73 (British XXX Corps), were given priority for receiving the new 17-pdr M10.

The scale of the Allied victory in Normandy greatly exceeded expectations. Allied commanders spent the four months after D-Day attempting to secure a decisive victory before they had assembled their full force. Neither the British-led Operation *Market Garden* (17–25 September) nor US operations around Aachen or in the Moselle delivered decisive victory in the face of German opposition, however, but once the Allies assembled their full force and logistics they and the Red Army had material superiority to overwhelm the Germans.

Allied planning was hampered by differences of opinion between General Dwight D. Eisenhower, commander of Supreme Headquarters Allied Expeditionary Force, and General Bernard L. Montgomery, commander of the Anglo-Canadian 21st Army Group, over the direction of strategy. Montgomery had been pressing for a single land forces commander and a concentration of force in northern Germany. This was only resolved after a serious crisis emerged at the end of the German Ardennes Offensive (16 December 1944–25 January 1945). Eisenhower asserted his authority and Montgomery and his Anglo-Canadian force became subsidiary to the main US effort.

Eisenhower set the direction for forthcoming operations with a directive on 20 January 1945. This was divided into three phases: '(1) The destruction of the German forces West of the Rhine and the closing of the Rhine. (2) The seizing of bridgeheads over the Rhine from which to develop operations into Germany. (3) The destruction of the German forces East of the Rhine and the advance into Germany.' These phases were then elaborated, with an estimate of the Allied and enemy forces expected.

At this stage of the war, Hitler's strategy was to buy time and hope for a miracle. Perhaps the Allies would fall out, as had the enemies of Hitler's hero Frederick the Great towards the end of the Seven Years' War (1756–63). A rational analysis of the German situation offered little hope. The last gambles in the West, the Ardennes and Alsace/Lorraine offensives, had failed. The remaining Axis armoured reserves were redeployed in a desperate attempt to retain control of the Hungarian oilfields. The Western Front had a lower priority for fuel and other resources than the East where the Germans were still attempting to halt the Soviet Vistula–Oder Operation (12 January–2 February 1945).

Hitler had insisted that the Western bank of the Rhine should be defended. As part of the defences of the area, the Germans planned to breach the Roer River dams in the

An Achilles of 75 AT Regt RA (11th Armoured Division) in the Netherlands, 12 October 1944. (Tank Museum 4389-D6)

Northern Eiffel mountains which would flood much of the west bank of the Rhine. Generalfeldmarschall Gerd von Rundstedt, the German Commander-in-Chief West, anticipated that the main attack by the 21st Army Group would be on the British Second Army Front between the Maas River and the Maas Bend. The Germans had identified developments south of Venlo, including new artillery positions and observation points, as well as the transport of construction materials. These may have been features of a British deception, however.

The battle of the Reichswald commenced on 8 February 1945. The 21st Army Group planned twin operations in the north, to start on 8 February from Nijmegen (Operation *Veritable*) and on 10 February from the Roer (Operation *Grenade*). The latter was to be mounted by the Ninth US Army (still under Montgomery's command), made up to ten divisions. Montgomery's directive for these Rhineland operations had been issued on 21 January and modified on 4 February. His intention was: 'To destroy all enemy in the area west of the Rhine from the present forward positions south of Nijmegen as far south as the general line Jülich–Dusseldorf, as a preliminary to crossing the Rhine and engaging the enemy in mobile war to the north of the Ruhr'. First Canadian Army, keeping its left wing on the Rhine, was to attack south-eastwards as far as the general line Xanten–Geldern (Operation *Veritable*); Ninth US Army, supported in the early stages by the left wing of 12th Army Group, was to attack north-eastwards with its right on the line Jülich–Dusseldorf (Operation *Grenade*); and British Second Army was to hold firm in the centre facing east.

At the beginning of February, the German front from near Nijmegen to about Roermond and from there to Jülich was held by General der Fallschirmtruppe Alfred Schlemm's 1. Fallschirm-Armee, part of Generaloberst Johannes Blaskowitz's Heeresgruppe H. Schlemm's army consisted of II. Fallschirm-Korps, LXXXVI. Armeekorps and LXIII. Armeekorps. About halfway between Venlo and Düsseldorf, XLVII. Panzerkorps was assembling, but the only German armour in the Reichswald was some 36 self-propelled heavy anti-tank guns; there were also about 100 artillery pieces.

COMBAT

D-DAY AND AFTER

On D-Day itself, the only significant German armoured attack took place in the Sword sector and was turned back by M4 Sherman tanks supported by 3in M10s. Although underemployed in the anti-tank role, M10s were extensively used as assault guns against bunkers and other German defences.

In the week following D-Day, the 17-pdr M10s of the British corps anti-tank regiments were heavily engaged against initial attempts by the 21. Panzer-Division, 12. SS-Panzer-Division and Panzer-Lehr-Division to drive the Allies back into the sea. During Operation *Perch* (7–14 June), 7th Armoured Division's 65 AT Regt RA fielded a number of 17-pdr M10s; these were employed in flank protection and played no part in the battle for Villers-Bocage on 13 June, but claimed at least one Tiger I knocked out during the German attacks on the divisional area.

At this time the first Jagdpanther-equipped battalion, schwere Panzerjäger-Abteilung 654, was still being re-formed as a Jagdpanther unit, having received orders to do so on 21 February 1944. Owing to production delays, however, the first vehicles received for training were Panther tanks. The first Jagdpanthers did not arrive until five vehicles were issued on 28 April, with a further 17 dispatched on 14 June 1944. As an interim measure, Stab/sPzJgAbt 654 was equipped with three Panther *Befehlswagen* (command tanks), while 1. and 2./sPzJgAbt 654 were expected to have 12 and 13 Jagdpanthers respectively. Shortly after midnight on 15 June 1944, however, 2./sPzJgAbt 654 left for the front with just eight vehicles. En route to Normandy and once there, the Jagdpanthers broke down almost continually due to a variety of mechanical problems. Although the battalion's formation progressed slowly, on

12 June 1944 OB West had requested a company be deployed to the Valognes area. This order was superseded by events on the battlefield and the eight were attached to the Panzer-Lehr-Division during 27–29 June, after which they were under the direct command of Panzergruppe West.

The Allied operations codenamed *Martlet* (25 June–1 July) and *Epsom* (26–30 June), both intended to seize the vital city of Caen from its German occupiers, coincided with the arrival of four more Panzer divisions in the Bayeux/Caen area, and an additional heavy tank battalion equipped with Tiger tanks. The British forces involved were the newly arrived VIII Corps, which included 91 AT Regt RA as its corps anti-tank regiment and the Guards and 11th Armoured divisions, each with two self-propelled anti-tank batteries in their anti-tank regiments (21 and 75 respectively). The British infantry-led assault was preceded by a rolling barrage and met by German counter-attacks conducted by armour and infantry. During the confused fighting, 17-pdr M10s played a significant part in defeating German armour. 91 AT Regt RA noted that the heavier weight of 17-pdr shot was needed to engage German armour at long range. M10s were also used as assault guns, blasting German snipers out of church towers.

During the next Allied effort to capture Caen, Operation *Charnwood* (8–9 July), 17-pdr M10s scored a major success against German armour. Two troops from 245 Bty (62 AT Regt RA) caught a group of Panther and PzKpfw IV tanks from SS-Panzer-Regiment 12 in the flank near Buron, claiming 13 tanks knocked out for the loss of four of their own vehicles (Copp 2004: 103–04, 296–97).

The next battles in the Caen area were the heavy fighting around Hill 112, a dominating feature south-west of Caen, during Operation *Jupiter* (10–11 July). The German forces included Tiger tanks, and 17-pdr guns were key. The lightly armoured and open-topped M10s suffered heavily from mortar and shell fire as well as armour-piercing shot. The British XII Corps anti-tank regiment, 86 AT Regt RA, claimed five Tigers but lost ten M10s.

Pictured in 1944, this knocked-out Jagdpanther has shed its tracks. Note the two-piece main-gun barrel. (ullstein bild via Getty Images)

The armour of the M10 was sufficient to keep out shell fragments and bullets but it was vulnerable to overhead airbursts or a direct hit from a mortar bomb in the open-topped turret. Officers in 17-pdr M10 troops were particularly vulnerable. Unlike armoured units in which the troop commander leads from a tank, an anti-tank troop commander was expected to command from the ground – as with field artillery. The troop commander was issued a Universal Carrier, but this vehicle was far from ideal, with poorer cross-country performance than the M10 and offering far less protection. During the first five weeks after D-Day, the 17-pdr M10-equipped 248 Bty (62 AT Regt RA) lost four out of its seven officers, three dead and one missing.

During July 1944, Crusader anti-aircraft tanks were phased out of armoured regiments. Some were acquired for use by the officers of self-propelled anti-tank batteries. Corps anti-tank regiments used Crusader gun tractors, so the expertise and spare parts to maintain these were available.

By this point schwere Panzerjäger-Abteilung 654 had reached Normandy, but there are no details about its use, apart from losing its first vehicle casualty to friendly fire and a second damaged by fire from a British anti-tank gun. During this time, 3./ PzJgAbt 654 was in transit by rail, taking 11 days to arrive and reaching the Normandy front on 18 July.

The next Allied assault was Operation *Goodwood* (18–20 July), which involved the armoured brigades of three armoured divisions (Guards, 7th and 11th) under British VIII Corps attacking from the bridgehead east of the Orne River. The Allied idea was to use armour to lead the attack to minimize casualties to the British and Canadian infantry. The assault was preceded by an aerial bombardment by hundreds of heavy and medium bombers with the intention of neutralizing the German defences in depth. The area east of Caen was congested and there was no space for VIII Corps' 91 AT Regt RA. In the event, the assault foundered on much deeper German anti-tank defences than anticipated with the loss of several hundred British tanks. The 17-pdr M10s took part in the armoured thrust, though they were used more as assault guns than in an anti-tank role. G Troop of 119 Bty (75 AT Regt RA, 11th Armoured Division) claimed two Panthers and a German Sherman. None of the anti-tank regiments involved in Operation *Goodwood* reported any losses of their M10s.

Operation *Goodwood* was the first of a series of Allied offensives employing massed bombers to neutralize German defences in depth before mounting a mechanized assault. These were the kinds of massed armoured assaults that the Jagdpanther-equipped heavy anti-tank battalions were intended to halt. Operation *Cobra* (25–31 July), mounted by the First US Army, took place in the close hedgerow country west of Saint-Lô, where it might have been difficult for the Jagdpanther to make best use of its long range. Similarly, the Jagdpanthers might have been effective in opposing the Allied operations codenamed *Totalize* (8–13 August) and *Tractable* (14–21 August), mounted by II Canadian Corps between Caen and Falaise, despite the use of night and smoke to screen Allied movement. These operations saw the Allied use of phalanxes of tanks and infantry mounted in improvised armoured personnel carriers over open rolling countryside. II Canadian Corps' 6 AT Regt RCA had landed in Normandy during 8–10 July; Operation *Totalize* was its first significant action. In preparation for this, armour plate was welded onto the turret tops of the regiment's M10s to provide some protection from overhead fire. The unit's self-

This heavily laden 17-pdr Achilles has a 'guest' in the turret whose headgear suggests he is from a Scottish unit. Note the Churchill infantry tank mudguard in the left foreground; Achilles often operated in support of Churchill-equipped armoured regiments in North-West Europe. (Tank Museum 3000-B5)

propelled guns were to advance behind the first groups of infantry and assist in holding captured positions until the arrival of towed guns; 56 Bty RCA lost four of its 12 guns in the fighting.

The only Jagdpanthers available were in British Second Army's sector, fighting amid much less favourable conditions. Before schwere Panzerjäger-Abteilung 654 could be deployed in the Caen–Falaise sector or against the torrent of US armour heading for Avranches, however, it was sucked into battle in the hedgerow country of Swiss Normandy between Vire and Falaise. This was in response to Operation *Bluecoat* (30 July–7 August 1944), British Second Army's effort to exploit the success of Operation *Cobra* and secure both Vire and Mont Pinçon. This action was the first in which the Jagdpanther and 17-pdr M10 could, and perhaps should, have met in combat.

On 30 July, the Churchill tank-equipped 6 Guards Tank Brigade, participating in its first action, was to support the infantry of 15th (Scottish) Infantry Division in an assault south from Caumont. In order to ease traffic congestion in Caumont, the 12

17-pdr M10 GUNSIGHT VIEW

R   L

The 17-pdr SP M10 was provided with an M51 direct-sighting telescope for direct fire, providing 3× magnification with a 13-degree field of view. This had a simple graticule with a horizontal scale covering the centre three degrees, with each numbered graduation being half a degree. Each degree subtends 17.5yd at 1,000yd. The approximately 3yd-wide Jagdpanther in the tree line fills just under 4 degrees in the sight, which means it is only a few hundred yards away. The flat trajectory of the QF 17-pdr means that there is little need to aim off for elevation at this short range and there would be a good chance of a hit even with Discarding Sabot Shot. This sight was replaced post-war with a tank sight engraved with range marks for different ammunition.

JAGDPANTHER GUNSIGHT VIEW

A view through a Jagdpanther's WZF 1/4 gunsight, targeting an Achilles at a far shorter range than recommended in the drill books. The sight provided 10× magnification with a 7-degree field of view. The Jagdpanther's binocular sight had only reticule lines in the left eyepiece and range scales in the left. The two images were superimposed when using both eyes. The reticles were 4 mils tall and 8 mils between the tops of the pyramids. A mil (*Strich*, in German) is the angle subtended by one metre at one kilometre. This helped the gunner to estimate the range to targets and to lay off for crossing targets. The range scales show the scale to apply for, from left to right, the Pzgr Patr 40/43 (HVAP, APCR), the Pzgr Patr 39/43 (APCBC-HE) and the Sprgr Patr 43 (HE).

17-pdr M10s of 146 Bty (91 AT Regt RA) were ordered away from the roads. The regiment's historian Desmond Flower noted that 'the possibilities of Churchill-M10 co-operation were at that time hardly dreamed of. Six months later we should have gone through together and the SPs would have covered the Churchills while they were working. But on this occasion we had nothing to do but sit like yokels beside the road and watch the traffic go through' (Flower 1950: 150). In 6 Guards Tank Brigade's first battle, cooperation between the arms broke down and a squadron of Churchills became isolated, occupying a ridge in front of the infantry. Less than 220yd away were three Jagdpanthers of schwere Panzerjäger-Abteilung 654, which knocked out 12 Churchills in a short space of time. While the British claimed to have damaged two of the Jagdpanthers, German records noted the loss of one *Befehlspanther*, when the final drives of Leutnant Scheiber's Jagdpanther were damaged. The vehicle could not be recovered due to strong enemy artillery fire and lack of towing vehicles. A further Jagdpanther suffered some kind of mechanical fault during the battle as the crew had reported a damaged drive sprocket some days previously.

On 4 August, 17-pdr M10s were engaged in their intended role when Q Bty, 21 AT Regt RA, was tasked with restoring the situation after a German battlegroup of Panther tanks and infantry from the 9. SS-Panzer-Division *Hohenstaufen* penetrated the Guards Armoured Division's gun area near Maisoncelle, inflicting losses of two self-propelled guns, two tanks and 21 soft-skinned vehicles of 153 Fd Regt RA. Q Bty had chosen a different approach to command and control, with troop and battery officers commanding from self-propelled guns as if they were tanks. The battery was organized into HQ, A and B troops. HQ Troop reached the area first, with the battery commander laying the gun on his self-propelled gun. The battery sergeant major's M10 was knocked out and he was killed. Three Panther tanks were knocked out before the Germans withdrew.

By the middle of August 1944, 2./sPzJgAbt 654's unit strength had dropped from 12 operational Jagdpanthers to just one. On 3 August, 1./sPzJgAbt 654 was declared

Officially designated the Panzer IV/70, the turretless tank destroyer based on the PzKpfw IV chassis and armed with the 7.5cm L/70 main gun served alongside the 7.5cm L/48-armed Jagdpanzer IV and the Jagdpanther in the anti-tank battalions of Germany's *Panzer* and *Panzergrenadier* divisions. (Imperial War Museums via Getty Images)

combat-ready, despite having just eight Jagdpanthers, and was ordered to Normandy. It travelled by rail as far as Châlons, and continued from there on its own tracks, reaching the front on 16 August as the German forces in France were in retreat. During the withdrawal to the Seine the battalion lost a total of 19 Jagdpanthers in defensive actions, but managed to cross the river with 28 serviceable vehicles – a higher number than most German armoured units. During the two months that schwere Panzerjäger-Abteilung 654 served in Normandy, Leutnant Günther Heyn of 2./sPzJgAbt 654 was credited with destroying at least nine Allied tanks.

The 17-pdr M10-equipped British and Canadian anti-tank regiments took part in the pursuit from Normandy. On 26–27 August, 6 AT Regt RCA supported the II Canadian Corps crossing of the Seine at Elbeuf.

A 17-pdr Achilles of 75 AT Regt RA (11th Armoured Division) with substantial foliage applied to it is pictured in action on 12 October 1944, engaging bunkers on the German border. (Tank Museum 3000-C3)

BEYOND NORMANDY

In early September, schwere Panzerjäger-Abteilung 559 was dispatched to the Western Front. This unit was formed in April 1944 and included one company of Jagdpanthers and two of *Sturmgeschütze*. Detraining at Tilburg, the commander, Major Erich Sattler, was ordered immediately to reinforce a German defensive position at Hechtel, with Luftwaffe troops including *Fallschirmjäger* guarding a valuable road intersection. Early on 8 September, Sattler's force, which included at least three Jagdpanthers, was surprised by Cromwell cruiser tanks of 2 Welsh Guards and Sattler's vehicle was quickly disabled, one of the Cromwells firing four rounds into the Jagdpanther's rear. (Sattler's Jagdpanther is now held at the Imperial War Museum, London.) Sattler himself, reportedly injured as he fell while exiting his vehicle, was able to evade capture and regain the German lines. At this time, schwere Panzerjäger-Abteilung 559 had nine Jagdpanthers on strength and took part in the attacks on the airborne corridor during Operation *Market Garden* (17–25 September). It remained in the Netherlands until December. Jagdpanthers were not being employed in the numbers and role envisaged, however.

First Canadian Army was tasked with clearing the Channel coast ports, and so 6 AT Regt RCA supported the attacks on Boulogne (17–22 September), Calais (25–30 September), the Breskens Pocket (6 October–3 November) and the island of Walcheren (1–8 November). With no tank threat, the Canadian anti-tank guns were employed exclusively as assault guns, developing procedures for cooperating with infantry that were recorded in their November 1944 war diary. On 23 November there was a demonstration of the accuracy and effectiveness of 17-pdr discarding-sabot ammunition against a captured Panther tank.

Jagdpanther units took part in operations against US Army units south of the British and Canadian sector. Schwere Panzerjäger-Abteilung 519, with 14 Jagdpanthers and 28 StuGs, joined I. SS-Panzerkorps in the defence of the Hürtgen Forest area, and took part in the Ardennes Offensive before being transferred to Alsace. Schwere Panzerjäger-Abteilungen 559 and 560 were attached to the Panzer-Lehr-Division and 12. SS-Panzer-Division respectively for the Ardennes fighting. Although on paper, 56 Jagdpanthers should have taken part, it appears that only 17 did. One action where Jagdpanthers appear to have been used in an anti-tank role was a doomed German attempt to prevent a column of US armour from relieving Bastogne at Assenois, just to the south of Bastogne, on 26 December. Although schwere Panzerjäger-Abteilung 654 did not take part in the Ardennes Offensive, it did support Operation *Nordwind* (31 December 1944–25 January 1945) in Alsace.

An Achilles of 75 AT Regt RA (11th Armoured Division) fires its 17-pdr gun at pillboxes on the German frontier, 12 October 1944. (Tank Museum 4389-D5)

OPERATIONS IN 1945

On 8 February 1945, Montgomery's 21st Army Group launched Operation *Veritable* to destroy the German forces between the Maas and Rhine rivers, seeking to clear the west bank of the Rhine before making the final assault into Germany. The operations was mounted by General H.D.G. Crerar's First Canadian Army with II Canadian and British XXX Corps.

Operation *Veritable*, also known as the Reichwald battles, took place between the Meuse and Rhine rivers. Natural obstacles and the weather as well as the presence of the enemy made this a challenging operation for the Allied forces. The terrain featured flooded areas and undulating woodlands. The Reichswald forest was key terrain, thick planted forest divided into blocks with sandy paths, while rising ground along the Rhine helped control flooding. The Canadian official historian described the battle area as gently rolling, largely arable land, ideal for armoured warfare if not for the wet conditions. The western edge was dominated by the Reichswald, a 13km by 6.5km forest filled with young pines and an inner belt of deciduous trees. Visibility varied greatly, complicating map-reading due to overgrown tracks and modified clearings. Only two paved roads traversed the forest north to south, restricting military movement along sandy rides.

The Reichswald sector of the German front was the responsibility of Generalmajor Heinz Fiebig's 84. Infanterie-Division, which formed the right wing of both General der Infanterie Erich Straube's LXXXVI. Armeekorps and General der Fallschirmtruppe Alfred Schlemm's 1. Fallschirmarmee. On Fiebig's right, across the Rhine, was the

Following Operation *Pheasant* (20 October–4 November 1944), the Allied effort to clear North Brabant in the wake of Operation *Market Garden*, soldiers from the Polish 1st Armoured Division examine a knocked-out Jagdpanther of schwere Panzerjäger-Abteilung 559 near the town of Langeweg in the Netherlands, November 1944. (Horace Abrahams/Keystone/Hulton Archive/Getty Images)

2. Fallschirm-Division of LXXXVIII. Armeekorps, 25. Armee. Established in Poland at the beginning of 1944, Fiebig's division had been made up of the remnants of exhausted infantry divisions and replacement units. It was almost entirely destroyed in the Falaise Pocket in August 1944. The division was reconstructed in September, and by the start of February 1945, had a strength of 10,000 mostly inexperienced troops who were insufficiently armed and equipped.

On 6 February, Fiebig was given Fallschirmjäger-Regiment 2 (2. Fallschirmjäger-Division), a well-equipped formation of 2,000 men recently drafted from the Luftwaffe. Fiebig had the Sicherungs-Bataillon Münster, a small unit of older men, and the 276. Magen (Stomach) Bataillon in reserve. The latter unit was made up of personnel whose chronic digestive issues made them unsuitable for active participation in defence. Fiebig's total artillery strength was approximately 100 guns. The only German armour in the Reichswald area were some 36 self-propelled assault guns of schwere Panzerjäger-Abteilung 655; 13 were Jagdpanthers, with the remainder a mix of *Sturmgeschütze* and Jagdpanzer IVs. At the start of the operation, this unit was forming in the Geldern area, south of the Reichswald.

The Germans had constructed three defensive belts across the region, marked by trenches and minefields, reinforcing villages and farmhouses as strongpoints. The foremost zone stretched across the western edge of the Reichswald. In the First Canadian Army's area of operations, this formidable outpost served as a barrier to the main Siegfried Line defences. It featured a double set of trenches, protected in front of the Reichwald by an anti-tank ditch.

First Canadian Army's plan was for a multi-phase assault. The first phase would be mounted by Lieutenant-General Sir B.G. Horrocks' British XXX Corps with the aim of clearing of the Reichswald and securing the line Gennep–Asperden–Kleve. After this, Lieutenant-General G.G. Simonds' II Canadian Corps was to be employed. The XXX Corps plan provided for the initial assault to be delivered on an

This Jagdpanther was knocked out by the US Army's 899th Tank Destroyer Battalion near Hargarten, Germany, in early March 1945. (US Army Signal Corps SC 421366)

11km (6.8-mile) front between the Maas and the Waal rivers by five infantry divisions; from right to left the 51st (Highland), 53rd (Welsh), 15th (Scottish) and the 2nd and 3rd Canadian. The first four would attack simultaneously at 1030hrs on D-Day; the 3rd Canadian Infantry Division's operations on the northern flank would not start before the evening. When 15th Infantry Division in the centre had secured an area of high ground known as the Materborn feature it was Horrocks' intention to bring forward the 43rd (Wessex) Infantry Division and the Guards Armoured Division from corps reserve and pass them through the gap to debouch into the open country south of Kleve, with the 43rd Infantry Division directed on Goch and the Guards on Uedem.

Three infantry divisions were to assault the Reichswald itself; from right to left/ south to north the 51st (Highland), 53rd (Welsh) and 15th (Scottish). Each would be supported by an armoured brigade. The 53rd (Welsh) Infantry Division had 34 Armoured Brigade, with 9th Royal Tank Regiment under command. These were equipped with Churchill tanks, which, unlike the Sherman- and Cromwell-armed brigades, did not include any 17-pdr-armed tanks within their establishment. To provide high-powered anti-tank guns, 56 AT Bty RCA, armed with 17-pdr SP M10 guns, was also placed under command.

The assaulting formations would be supported by unusually large artillery resources, for Horrocks was determined to blast a way into the German defences with gunfire. In the interests of maintaining surprise, however, the guns would not fire until the morning of the attack. The fire plan was required to provide for an immense though brief artillery preparation programme that would prevent any German interference with the initial assault; complete saturation of the German defences and the destruction or neutralization of their concrete emplacements; then immediate supporting fire for the attacking infantry and armour, and the employment of the medium and heavy guns in such a way as to cover the deep penetration to the Materborn feature without involving the batteries in any major moves.

Achilles supporting 15th (Scottish) Infantry Division assemble for Operation *Veritable*, 8 February 1945. The vehicles on the left of the image are 17-pdr Archer self-propelled guns, which replaced many towed equipments in the divisional anti-tank regiments during 1945. (Tank Museum 3000-B3)

Weather permitting, Operation *Veritable* was to benefit from air support on the maximum scale. The air plan provided for both pre-planned and impromptu air support from heavy and medium bombers and fighter-bombers.

Every effort was made by the Allied troops to gain surprise during the operation. A cover plan was put in place to divert the enemy's attention towards Lieutenant-General Sir J.T. Crocker's British I Corps, which was located some way to the west. The real battlefront was carefully concealed, and strict security measures were enforced during the administrative build-up. No movement during daylight hours was allowed east of the 's-Hertogenbosch–Helmond Canal, except for reconnaissance parties. These parties had to remove their formation patches from their battledress and cross the Maas in Canadian vehicles, accompanied by Canadian liaison officers.

As the assaulting formations moved from their places of concentration to the forward assembly areas, an elaborate camouflage programme was devised to hide the large concentration of artillery in the areas to the east and south of Nijmegen, as well as the huge quantities of stores, ammunition and petrol involved in the pre-battle dumping programme. XXX Corps vehicles had their identifying divisional signs removed to conceal their movements further.

According to the formation's post-action report, the troops of 53rd (Welsh) Infantry Division considered themselves well prepared for Operation *Veritable*. During the previous month they had seen service in forested areas of the Ardennes and in extreme cold, and had adapted their tactics to suit woodland operations. A battalion would advance on a single axis, one company up, as attempts to operate on a wider front risked loss of control.

Operation *Veritable*'s opening fire plan started at 2200hrs on 7 February with heavy bombers dropping 1,397 tons of bombs on the town of Kleve and 475 tons of bombs

Airborne troops, possibly Canadian, hitch a ride on a 17-pdr Achilles in the Minden sector, April 1945. The tam o'shanter worn by the No. 1 suggests this might be a vehicle of 91 AT Regt RA. (Tank Museum 3000-C1)

on the defensive positions and roads at Goch. A programme of artillery fire from 1,050 artillery guns started at 0730hrs and continued throughout 8 February, targeting German infantry, artillery and mortar positions.

On 8 February, 2. and 3./sPzJgAbt 655 moved north to the Kleve area, arriving at daybreak on 9 February. Their vehicles were refuelled and took up positions in support of the infantry. The German anti-tank guns were deployed to cover exits from the Reichswald where they had a big enough field of fire and where they would not be at risk of being overrun by enemy infantry infiltrating through the Reichswald.

The advance conducted by 53rd (Welsh) Infantry Division was on a narrow front, with the initial break-in by 71 Infantry Brigade taking the first line of defences and 160 Infantry Brigade taking the lead to assault the Siegfried Line defences; they reached their start line at 0200hrs on 9 February. As the leading British columns advanced with their axis on a single track, there was little German opposition, but the ground soon became a quagmire, and all vehicles other than tanks became bogged down. German opposition typically consisted of groups of 40–50 infantry supported by one or more self-propelled guns sited to shoot along the tracks. Two troops of 56 Bty RCA advanced with 2nd Battalion, The Monmouthshire Regiment. The battery commander, Captain Whalley, mounted in an M5 Honey light tank, took 30 prisoners after shots were fired from the tank's 37mm gun and Browning machine guns.

On 9 February, 2 Monmouthshire came under heavy fire from two German self-propelled guns north of the Reichswald. Immediately, and without seeking cover for

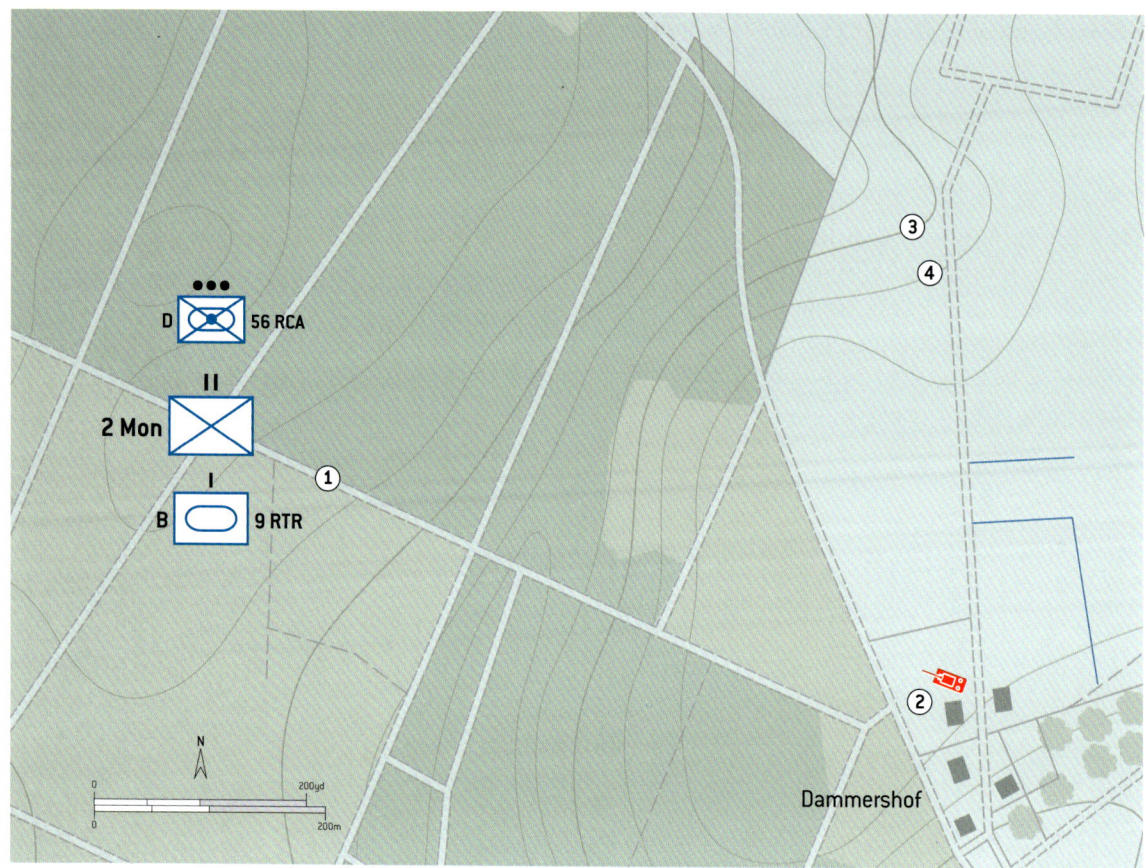

This map shows the action in which an Achilles of Lieutenant Charles Kydd's D Tp, 6 AT Regt RCA, stalked and knocked out a Jagdpanther of sPzJgAbt 655 near Kleve on 11 February 1945. After 2 Monmouthshire, moving along one of the lateral roads (**1**), came under fire from a high-velocity gun (**2**), Kydd advanced on foot and crawling until he reached a position (**3**) from where he could see the enemy vehicle. Kydd then led one of his 17-pdr M10s to a position (**4**) from where the German self-propelled gun could be engaged. Four shots hit and did not penetrate the vehicle, but knocked off a track and a vision bloc and prompted the five-man crew to bale out. A Churchill tank of 9 RTR then took the German crewmen prisoner.

his troop, Lieutenant C.H. Kydd ordered his guns to engage the enemy. Both German vehicles were put out of action and 2 Monmouthshire continued the advance. The enemy were identified as parachute infantry from Fallschirmjäger-Regimenter 19 and 20 of the 7. Fallschirmjäger-Division.

Saturday 10 February was a quiet day for 2 Monmouthshire, with another battalion taking the lead. On 11 February, 2 Monmouthshire took the lead, crossing the start line at 0900hrs with the objective being a road junction where their track crossed the main lateral road, about 1,500m from the far end of the Reichswald. There was heavy opposition from German machine guns and hand-held anti-tank weapons. This operation lasted until 1000hrs and cost the battalion 40 casualties. Two 17-pdr M10s of D Troop were hit by *Panzerfaüste* but not knocked out. One gunner was killed and a sergeant and gunner were wounded, but the guns remained in action. Meanwhile, schwere Panzerjäger-Abteilung 655 was ordered to mount a counter-attack towards Materborn, south of Kleve. The Jagdpanthers and Jagdpanzers struggled with track trouble in the heavy going, with at least one Jagdpanther abandoned and the crew taken prisoner after becoming disoriented. A Jagdpanther advanced on 2 Monmouthshire, but withdrew east when it came under fire from the M10s.

A little later, 2 Monmouthshire came under heavy and accurate fire from a German high-velocity gun and the battalion was held up. Lieutenant Kydd moved his troop to a covered position and set out on foot to establish the position of the enemy gun. He crawled under fire from small arms and mortars, to the top of a rise from which he could see the enemy vehicle, later identified as a 'Jadpanther'. He then returned to his troop, selected an anti-tank gun, commanded by Sergeant J.J. Crafton, and led it over exceptionally difficult ground and under fire to a position on the enemy's flank. From here he knocked out the 'Jadpanther' with four rounds, clearing the way for 2 Monmouthshire to continue its advance. The M10s seem to have been followed by a troop of Churchill tanks from 9 RTR led by Lieutenant T.C. Fawcett MC, who captured the five Jagdpanther crew members who had taken shelter in the farm.

On 12 February, still in support of 2 Monmouthshire, Kydd's D Troop knocked out another enemy self-propelled gun by quick and accurate shooting. Throughout the operation, Kydd showed an extraordinary determination to come to grips with the enemy. His rapid appreciation of a situation and his ability to deal with it immediately were deemed to be outstanding. The effectiveness with which he fought his guns contributed in no small measure to the success of the operation in which he was engaged. Thus ended one of the few, if not the only duel between the 17-pdr SP M10 guns and the Jagdpanther.

Photographed on 16 March 1945, Private W.G. Lourie examines a Jagdpanther put out of action by a 17-pdr gun of 6 AT Regt RCA in the Reichswald, Germany. This may be the wreck from the 11 February action described in this chapter. (Library and Archives Canada, MIKAN 3203401)

STATISTICS AND ANALYSIS

On paper the Jagdpanther was far superior to the 17-pdr SP M10. In the balance between firepower, protection and mobility, the Jagdpanther was optimized for firepower and protection. While on paper the Jagdpanther had reasonable tactical mobility, however, its mobility was undermined by problems of reliability. There is a suspicion that the reported reduction in mechanical failures may have been due to the crews learning to operate within the constraints of their vehicles. These included avoiding over-revving the engine, neutral turns, or turns in reverse or in soft ground to preserve the transmission. If the engine stalled, the driver had to pause before trying to restart the engine. Otherwise, petrol leaving from a flooded engine would be apt to catch fire with potentially disastrous consequences.

The Jagdpanther's 8.8cm gun had superior accuracy and power and could penetrate any British or US AFV at 2,000m range. Its frontal armour would defeat 17-pdr APCBC shot at most ranges and the poor accuracy of 17-pdr APDS shot was such that it was inadvisable to engage a target at ranges greater than 600yd. Had the conditions on the Western Front been similar to those in the East, where AFV combat could take place at long range, the Jagdpanther would have enjoyed a decisive advantage. Instead, typical engagement ranges in North-West Europe were less than 800m. In mobile phases of war, the Jagdpanther's lack of operational mobility was a disadvantage.

Although on paper the Jagdpanther was a superior tank destroyer, during the battle for the Reichswald it was outfought by the 17-pdr M10 self-propelled guns. The Jagdpanther involved was on its own, contrary to German tactical doctrine, and engaged by a troop rather than a single AFV; the 17-pdr M10's success can be attributed to the skilful and brave actions of the officer who led his troop on foot. Perhaps that is typical

This 17-pdr Achilles, date, unit and location unknown, appears to have been knocked out while in transit. Note the debris partly covering the Achilles, the huge crater in the foreground and the vehicle moving past it, presumably along a road. (Tank Museum 3000-C4)

of the experience of the Jagdpanther. At no point during the campaign in North-West Europe were Jagdpanthers available in the numbers that would allow them to be used in the way envisaged by German tactical doctrine. Indeed, on 11 February 1945, schwere Panzerjäger-Abteilung 655 was committed to a counter-attack individually as assault guns, firmly against doctrine. This was the pattern for the Jagdpanther units fielded on the Western Front, from eight Jagdpanthers of schwere Panzerjäger-Abteilung 654 flung into battle, to Major Sattler's counter-attack and the self-propelled guns lost in the Ardennes Offensive. One reflection of the experience of the soldiers who manned the Jagdpanther is in the title of the memoir by Franz Kopka recounting the experiences of schwere Panzerjäger-Abteilung 559 – 'Missbraucht und gebeutelt' – which translates as 'abused and battered'. Kopka was a highly decorated veteran officer of that unit.

The 17-pdr M10 was a British improvisation using the interim design of tank destroyer. It was probably the most effective Allied tank destroyer on the Western Front and used extensively as an assault gun in a secondary role, despite the School of Artillery's doctrinal reservations about its offensive use. The aggressive employment of the 17-pdr M10 was perhaps closer to the original US Army tank-destroyer concept, however.

The British converted 1,017 of the 1,500 Lend-Lease M10s to 17-pdr M10s. By comparison, 2,000 M4 Sherman tanks were armed with 17-pdr guns to become Fireflys. Roughly one-third of British AFVs armed with a gun capable of taking on the heavier German tanks were M10s. The 17-pdr M10 was a much more significant part of Britain's anti-tank weaponry than the Jagdpanther was of the German armour force. A total of just 415 Jagdpanthers were built, compared to some 6,000 Panther tanks, making the Jagdpanther a rare beast.

One area where the performance of the guns was very different was in the accuracy of each equipment.

8.8cm PaK 43 accuracy								
Round		Range						
		100m	500m	1,000m	1,500m	2,000m	2,500m	3,000m
8.8cm Pzgr 40/43	Training	100%	100%	100%	97%	89%	78%	66%
	Action	100%	100%	89%	66%	47%	34%	25%

Photographed in 2011, this Jagdpanther is housed at the Musée des Blindes in Saumur, France. The one-piece barrel and *Zimmerit* show this is an early Jagdpanther. The rear idler exhibits battle damage. Although the provenance is unknown, it is possible that this was one of the sPzJgAbt 654 vehicles lost in France. (Matthia Hllander/ Wikimedia/CC0)

17-pdr accuracy*					
Probability (%) of hitting a static hull-up target with first round:					
Range	500yd	1,000yd	1,500yd	2,000yd	2,500yd
Line	100%	100%	100%	98%	93%
Range	98%	46%	20%	10%	5%
both (hit)	98%	46%	20%	10%	5%
Probability (%) of hitting static hull-up target after first round:					
Range	500yd	1,000yd	1,500yd	2,000yd	2,500yd
both (hit)	100%	94%	71%	50%	26%
Probability (%) of hitting moving target (direct-crossing at 15mph) after first round:					
Range	500yd	1,000yd	1,500yd	2,000yd	
	86%	48%	26%	16%	
Probability (%) of hitting hull-down target with first round:					
Range	500yd	1,000yd	1,500yd	2,000yd	
	59%	18%	26%	16%	
Probability (%) of hitting static hull-down target after first round:					
Range	500yd	1,000yd	1,500yd	2,000yd	2,500yd
	88%	51%	29%	18%	12%

* Target assumed to be the size of a PzKpfw VI Tiger tank. Source: WO 291/180, Operations Research report on accuracy of anti-tank gunnery.

One of the main conclusions was that the major reason for the low probability of a first-round hit was the difficulty estimating the range. Once a first round could be seen on the ground, artillery bracketing drills would achieve a hit given sufficient ammunition. This is where the stereoscopic rangefinder of the Jagdpanther was a big advantage. British wartime analysis of tank losses concluded that it was impossible to armour a tank sufficiently to defeat a round from the latest high-velocity guns. It was considered better to put a bigger gun on a tank and improve the odds of a first-round kill. The Jagdpanther anticipated the post-war trend towards increasingly sophisticated fire-control equipment.

AFTERMATH

Charles Kydd continued in command of D Troop, 56 Bty RCA, until 26 February 1945. It was a bad day for the battery, with its anti-tank guns attracting shells and mortar bombs. While Kydd rallied his troop his M5 Stuart light tank struck a mine.

This Dutch Achilles pictured in 1950 is named 'Tijger' (Tiger). (Leger Film- en Fotodienst/ Wikimedia/CC0)

Kydd was wounded in the leg by shrapnel. His driver was badly wounded in both legs while the other two crew members were evacuated with shock. The tank remained under mortar fire for some time before the wounded could be evacuated. That was Charles Kydd's last action of the war. He was awarded the Military Cross for his skill and courage between 8 and 15 February, the citation for his medal mentioning that his 'rapid appreciation of a situation and his ability were outstanding. His personal courage and presence of mind were a source of a great inspiration to his own men and to other troops.'

Although using 17-pdr SP M10s to support Churchill-armed tank brigades seemed to work, at the end of the Reichswald operation the Corps Commander Royal Artillery of II Canadian Corps, Brigadier P.A.S. Todd, expressed a wish that his corps anti-tank regiments should be confined to their proper role and not deployed in the forward defensive lines. Elsewhere in 21st Army Group, however, the 17-pdr SP M10 was used extensively in the assault gun role. Several developments for the 17-pdr supported its role as an assault gun. An Improved high-explosive round was developed with a reduced charge, reducing barrel wear.

A British crew tasked with assessing a Jagdpanther after war's end. None of the Jagdpanthers and Panthers tested by the British after the war completed the standard acceptance tests for British AFVs, highlighting the technical fragility of the design. (Tank Museum 0567-F5)

The 17-pdr SP M10 was retained with the Royal Armoured Corps after the end of World War II and was fitted with the Royal Armoured Corps tank telescope. Better APDS was available post-war, which improved accuracy.

The concept of a lightly armoured, heavily armed tank destroyer was continued by the British Charioteer. This vehicle was intended to operate with armoured units still equipped with Cromwell tanks which were retained owing to the slow production of Centurion main battle tanks. The Charioteer mounted an Ordnance QF 20-pdr (84mm) high-velocity gun in a two-man turret on a Cromwell tank chassis. Its features almost match the wish list of M10 modifications drawn up by the 17-pdr SP M10 gunners in Normandy: it had an enclosed turret and a coaxial machine gun. Only a small number of Charioteers were produced, however, with surplus vehicles sold overseas. The vehicle was not well regarded by the Royal Armoured Corps and it features in the Tank Museum's tank chats as one of 'the worst-ever British tanks'; but this may say more about the culture of the Royal Armoured Corps and its mantra that the best anti-tank weapon is another tank.

The Jagdpanther remained in service during the rest of World War II. The post-war Bundeswehr retained the concept of a turretless tank destroyer in the 90mm *Kanonenjagdpanzer* or *Jagdpanzer Kanone*. Weighing 27.5 tons, it was closer conceptually to the Jagdpanzer IV than the heavier Jagdpanther. Post-war conclusions were that there was no point in a super-heavily armoured tank destroyer as post-war tank guns would overmatch any level of armour. With the development of wire-guided anti-tank missiles in the 1960s the concept of self-propelled anti-tank guns fell out of favour.

A three-quarters view of the Weald Foundation's preserved Jagdpanther, 2024. The chassis number of this rebuilt vehicle is not known. It is finished in the colours and markings of a Jagdpanther of the 116. Panzer-Division in March 1945. (Weald Foundation)

BIBLIOGRAPHY

Anderson, T. (2018). *The History of the Panzerjäger, Volume 1: Origins and Evolution 1939–42*. Oxford: Osprey Publishing.

Anderson, T. (2020). *The History of the Panzerjäger, Volume 2: From Stalingrad to Berlin 1943–45*. Oxford: Osprey Publishing.

Anonymous (1946). *History of the 6th Canadian Anti-tank Regiment, Royal Canadian Artillery, 1st April, 1942–24th June, 1945*.

Boscawan, R. (2000). *Armoured Guardsman: A War Diary, June 1944–April 1945*. Barnsley: Pen & Sword.

Copp, T. (2004). *Fields of Fire: The Canadians in Normandy*. Toronto: University of Toronto Press.

Department of the Army (1946). *The Tank Destroyer*. History Study No. 29 I 3. DTIC. Historical Section, Army Ground Forces.

Department of the Army (1953). *German Explosive Ordnance (Projectiles and Projectile Fuzes)*. TM 9-1985-3/ TO 39B-1A-10.

Dörr, M. (2011). *So kämpfte die 654: Schwere Panzerjäger-Abteilung 654*. Zweibrücken: VDM Heinz Nickel.

Doyle, D. (2016). *M10/Achilles: A Visual History of the US Army's WWII Tank Destroyer*. Memphis, TN: Ampersand Group.

Ellis, L.F. et al. (1968). *Victory in the West, Volume 2: The Defeat of Germany*. London: HMSO.

Flower, D. (1950). *The History of the Argyll & Sutherland Highlanders 5th Battalion: 91st Anti-Tank Regiment 1939–1945*. London: Thomas Nelson.

Foulds, Tony (1998). 'In Support of the Canadians: A British Anti-Tank Regiment's First Five Weeks in Normandy', *Canadian Military History* 7.2: 71–78. Available at https://core.ac.uk/download/303918740.pdf (accessed 27 August 2024).

Graves, D.E. (2013). *Blood and Steel: The Wehrmacht Archive, Normandy 1944*. Barnsley: Frontline Books.

Jentz, Thomas L. (1997). *Jagdpanzer 38 to JagdTiger*. Panzer Tracts 9. Hagerstown, MD: Darlington Productions.

Jentz, Thomas L. (2004). *Germany's Panther Tank: The Quest for Combat Supremacy, Development Modifications, Rare Variants, Characteristics, Combat Accounts*. Atglen, PA: Schiffer Publishing.

Kropka, F.M. (1999). *Missbraucht und gebeutelt 1939-1945: Schicksal einer selbständigen Einheit Schwerer Panzerjäger als Heerestruppe*. FPNr. 10509.

Moran, Nicholas (2020). *Can Openers: The Development of American Anti-tank Gun Motor Carriages*. Brattleboro, VT: Echo Point.

Münch, K.-H. (2002). *The Combat History of schwere Panzerjäger-Abteilung 654: In Action in the East and West with the Ferdinand and the Jagdpanther*. Winnipeg: J.J. Fedorowicz.

Nafziger, George (n.d.). 'German Army Authorized Strength Staff Company Heavy Panzerjäger 'Jagdpanther' Company (Freie Gliederung), 1 March 1944'. Available at https://usacac.army.mil/sites/default/files/documents/carl/nafziger/944GQEU.pdf (accessed 27 August 2024).

Nicholson, G.W.L. (1967). *The Gunners of Canada: The History of the Royal Regiment of Canadian Artillery 1534–1967*. Two volumes. Toronto: McClelland & Stewart.

Oliver, D. (2017). *Jagdpanther Tank Destroyer: German Army and Waffen SS Western Europe 1944–1945*. Tankcraft 8. Barnsley: Pen & Sword.

Pemberton, A.L. (1951). *The Development of Artillery Tactics and Equipment*. London: HMSO.

Royal Armoured Corps (1952). 'Training, Volume III: Armament. SP 17-pr M10'. Pamphlet No. 7. War Office.

Saunders, T. (2023). *The Battle of the Reichswald: Rhineland February 1945*. Barnsley: Pen & Sword.

Spielberger, Walter J. (2004). *Panther & Its Variants*. Atglen, PA: Schiffer.

Stacey, Colonel C.P. (1960). *Official History of the Canadian Army in the Second World War, Volume III: The Victory Campaign: The Operations in North-West Europe, 1944–1945*. Ottawa: National Defence.

Townend, W. & Baldwin, F. (2020). *Gunners in Normandy: The History of the Royal Artillery in North West Europe, January 1942 to August 1944*. Stroud: The History Press.

War Office (1945). 'HQ BAOR: Notes on Operations of 21 Army Group 6 June 1944–8 May 1945'.

War Office (1946a). 'Gun drill for Q.F. 17-pr, Mark 1 gun on carriage 17-pr, Mark 1'.

War Office (1946b). 'Maintenance manual for the ordnance, Q.F. 17-pr., Mark 1 on carriage, 17-pr., Marks 1 and 1W and ordnance, Q.F. 17-pr., Mark 5 on 3-inch gun motor carriage, M10: land service'.

War Office (1946c). 'User Handbook 17-pr., Marks 1 and 1W and ordnance, Q.F. 17-pr., Mark 5 on 3-inch gun motor carriage, M10 : land service'.

Watertown Arsenal Laboratory (1945a). 'Experimental Report 710/715: Metallurgical Examination of a 3¼in. Thick Armor Plate from a German PzKw V (Panther) Tank'.

Watertown Arsenal Laboratory (1945b). 'Experimental Report 710/750: Metallurgical Examination of Armor and Welded Joints from the Side of a German PzKw V (Panther) Tank'.

Wedemeyer, A.C. (1941). 'Antitank Defense', *Field Artillery Journal* 31: 258–72.

WO 219/2806, Appx G to SHAEF/16652/GCT/Arty, 11 July 1944.

WO 373-54-19. Medal Citation for Charles Hewson Kydd.

Zaloga, S.J. (2002). *M10 and M36 Tank Destroyers 1942–53*. New Vanguard 57. Oxford: Osprey Publishing.

Zetterling, Niklas (2000). *Normandy 1944*. Winnipeg: J.J. Fedorowicz.

Zetterling, Niklas (2018a). 'Repair of Jagdpanthers at Normandy – Part I'. Available at https://www.dupuyinstitute.org/blog/2018/08/01/repair-of-jadgpanthers-at-normandy-part-i/ (accessed 24 August 2024).

Zetterling, Niklas (2018b). 'Repair of Jagdpanthers at Normandy – Part II'. Available at https://www.dupuyinstitute.org/blog/2018/08/02/repair-of-jagdpanthers-at-normandy-part-ii/ (accessed 24 August 2024).

WAR DIARIES

2nd Battalion, The Monmouthshire Regiment
6th Anti-Tank Regiment, Royal Canadian Artillery
9th Royal Tank Regiment
53rd (Welsh) Infantry Division
160 Infantry Brigade
XXX Corps

The Dammenhof farmhouse in 2024. The duel took place in front of the farmhouse, which still shows splinter and bullet damage from the action. [Edwin Popken]

INDEX